Design

Sourcebook

CERAMICS

EDMUND DE WAAL

NEW HOLLAND

CONTENTS

INTRODUCTION

Ceramics are unlike the other arts. We feel we know ceramics, we

handle them everyday, we welcome them into our domestic lives and place them at the centre of our

rituals. They are often an unremarked constant in the background of our days. But they are a Trojan Horse,

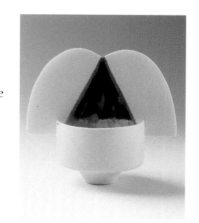

planting a reminder of a profound transformative process in the midst of the continuity. This

process, the changing of common clay into something strange and other, is at the heart of our

myths of making. Adam, after all, was made from clay. Fired clay, malleable earth made

hard through its interaction with fire, is all around us, geologically, historically,

architecturally and, increasingly, technologically. The art of ceramics, however deeply it is

buried, still retains the pulse of this change, a memory of this bridging of two

states of being. This means that everything from porcelain coffee cup to figurative

sculpture shares a basic metaphorical language. Some of the richness of this

language is unfolded in this book.

The twentieth century revival of interest in hand–made

and decorated pottery is described as the studio ceramics

movement. There are many divergent figures within this

movement but there is a shared interest in the qualities and ideas that can be found in pottery.

This is a book for makers and students, for collectors and users of studio ceramics – a

sourcebook of ideas and images. It has been divided into chapters, not of competing

schools of artists but of general approaches to ideas. It cannot hope to be comprehensive:

it is a very personal selection of work that I find beautiful, intriguing, moving or even

funny. Much of it is very different from the kind of ceramics that I make. But one of the

real joys of ceramics is just that exhilarating breath of difference, the sense of ambiguous and

continuous reinvention that is a marker for art.

EDMUND DE WAAL

CLEAR
CONSTRUCTION

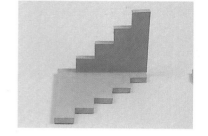

MANY POTTERS ARE INTRIGUED **by**

simple forms and clear construction, finding that there is great

subtlety to be explored within these parameters. One of the pleasures of

these ceramics is that they seem to tell you how they were made. When you

have them in your hands, the story of their making unfolds: whether quick

or laborious, unstudied or complex, the process of their creation and the

process of handling them come together. In this way, less is very often more.

⬥ **Cargo Dishes (detail). Edmund de Waal.**
Porcelain, celadon glazes. Max. ⌀ 38 cm
(15 in). 1997

These dishes have strong profiles that are
distorted through gentle warping. The edges
of the dishes are left unglazed to accentuate
them and to contrast with the celadon.

⬥ **Cut-outs (detail). Ken Eastman.**
White stoneware clay, coloured slips and
oxides. Slab built and painted, fired several
times at 1800°C. 16 x 16 x 16 cm
(6¼ x 6¼ x 6¼ in). 1998

Eastman explores shadows and angles in his
constructed pieces.

⬥ **Dish. Julian Stair.** Stoneware. Thrown
and constructed. ⌀ 62 cm (24½ in). 1998

Constructed from thrown elements, this large
dish is a striking example of balance and
tension between contrasting shapes. The
spiral in the middle of the dish, made during
the throwing, contrasts with the almost
architectural precision of the rim.

THE NEW AUSTERITY

There have always been simple pots. Sometimes their simplicity

reflected a particular ceremonial use, as in the white glazed pots

used on Chinese altars. Sometimes, as with the fiercely plain

ceramics of Henry Cole in Victorian England or the pottery of the

Bauhaus, they displayed a strongly negative

attitude towards ornamentation. Sometimes it was

just the speed of the making of a pot that

necessitated simplicity. But more often austerity is

a reflection of a belief that the form of a pot is

primary and that glazes, surfaces and decoration

should not overwhelm it. This is not an aridly conceptual view of

form, rather it is a rich, and sometimes seductive, way of exploring

form. It is an approach that is regaining momentum: it is a new

austerity that finds a counterpart in contemporary minimalist

architecture and sculpture. These pots show that it is possible to

make work that resonates with the past, yet is truly challenging.

Still Life, Two Bottles, Goblet and Beaker. Gwyn Hanssen Pigott. Porcelain. Max. height 27.5 cm (10¾ in). 1992

The way in which the shadows intersect between the pots in this group has been given particular attention.

Vase. Rob Barnard. Stoneware, naturally occurring ash glaze. Anagama-fired. 22 x 14 cm (8¾ x 5½ in). 1997

Fired using wood in a Japanese-style kiln, the beauty of this pot depends on the tension between the random markings from the flame and the deliberate clarity of line of the thrown form.

Platter with Handles. Takeshi Yasuda. Creamware/hi-temp earthenware. Ø 32 cm (26¾ in). 1998

Yasuda exploits the plasticity of the clay with great dexterity. The two handles distort the roundness of the platter, creating a vortex of spiralling movement.

Milk Jug and Sauce Boat. Takeshi Yasuda. Creamware/hi-temp earthenware. Jug: 17 x 8 x 11 cm (6¾ x 3¼ x 4¼ in). Sauce boat: 13 x 12 x 18 cm (5¼ x 4¾ x 7 in). 1997

These pots seem thrown almost to the point of collapse – lips seem impossibly thin and forms impossibly stretched. The handles are playful and challenge the user to handle the pot in unexpected ways.

12

Plateau with Handles. Takeshi Yasuda. Creamware/hi-temp earthenware. Ø 34 cm (13½ in). 1998

This is a pot for the display of food that also manages to echo archaic Chinese bronze ritual vessels, through its applied handles. One of Yasuda's strengths is that his pots are historically resonant in this subtle way.

Bowl with a Handle. Takeshi Yasuda. Creamware/hi-temp earthenware. Large bowl: Ø 40 cm (16 in). Small bowls: Ø 24 cm (9½ in). 1998

These domestic pots work well when handled, used and stacked; the vestigial handles giving a sense of security. All these pots have a soft cream glaze that looks both to eighteenth-century English creamwares and to Chinese stoneware glazes, yet is distinctly contemporary in its austerity.

Turquoise Bowl. Alev Ebüzziya Siesbye.
Stoneware. Hand-built. 9 x 12 cm (3½ x 4¾ in).
1997

*Saturated colour is a hallmark of Siesbye's work.
Her bowls have the depth of colours of Islamic
ceramics; the drenched tonality comes from the
light-absorbing matt surfaces of her glazes.*

(Untitled) (detail). Alev Ebüzziya Siesbye.
Stoneware. Hand-built. ∅ 25 cm (9¾ in). 1996

*The rim of this bowl, with its sgraffito line
revealing the exposed clay beneath the glaze,
shows how adept Siesbye is at creating visual
tension between the interior and exterior.*

**Sky Blue Bowl with Lapis Lazuli Rim.
Alev Ebüzziya Siesbye.** Stoneware. Hand-
built. 8 x 10 cm (3¼ x 4 in). 1997

*The slight change of direction in rim
and foot echo each other, setting up a
complex visual dynamic. Siesbye's bowls
give the vertiginous sense that they have
actually levitated.*

**Sealmark Detail.
Edmund de Waal.**

*These impressed marks are a
mixture of old seals and
found objects. The glaze is a
celadon, reminiscent of
Korean and Chinese glazes.*

**Large Lidded Jar.
Edmund de Waal.** Porcelain.
Thrown. Max. height 42 cm
(16½ in). 1998

*The shallow ribs on this
large lidded jar mark out its
proportions. Sealmarks are
applied, then the pot is
dented so that there is no
obvious front or back.*

Bottle Vases. Edmund de Waal. Porcelain. Thrown. Max. height
32 cm (12½ in) high. 1997

*These bottle vases were made as a pair to sit close to each other. They
were thrown precisely, then gently knocked to indent them. This
asymmetry means that they fit easily into the hand.*

Teapot. Edmund de Waal. Porcelain and galvanized wire. Thrown.
Max. height 28 cm (11 in). 1997

*The skirt of this teapot was thrown, then torn to give a "running"
edge. The combination of steel wire and porcelain seemed pleasingly
incongruous: a cheap material in conjunction with a precious one.*

This porcelain cup and saucer are so well visually balanced that it is difficult to register the complexity of their making. Fine judgements as to how the cup sits within the saucer mean the cup seems to float. The surface of the white glaze Constantinidis uses is smooth and matt, making her pots seductive to use.

Slender Mug. Joanna Constantinidis. Porcelain. Thrown. Height 11 cm (4¼ in). 1998

Constantinidis' use of porcelain is very controlled: all marks of throwing and turning are absent. This mug is as much an exercise in proportion as it is a drinking vessel.

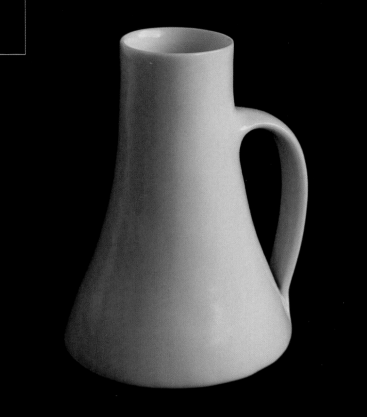

Tilted Bowl. Joanna Constantinidis. Porcelain. Thrown, pared and burnished. 10 x 15 cm (4 x 6 in). 1997

This is a thrown bowl that has been cut off the wheel at an angl and altered. It was burnished, then fired in a saggar to give it a lustrous and rich surface. This off-centre form plays with ideas and expectations of balance.

Two White Bowls with Saucers. Rupert Spira. Stoneware. Thrown. Left cup: ⌀ 9 cm (3½ in). Right cup: ⌀ 8 cm (3¼ in). 1998

Spira's pots are poised and elegant. These bowls with their severe profiles are reminiscent of Modernist ceramics from the 1920s.

Matt Black and White Oval Shape Vases. Rupert Spira. Stoneware. Thrown. Left: height 22 cm (8½ in). Right: height 23 cm (9 in). 1998

Spira uses an extraordinarily wide palette of glazes but here he employs just two, one shiny and one matt, in an almost illustrative way. These pots depend for their success on the tension at the rim between the different glazes.

THE NEW AUSTERITY

◻ **Limoges
Porcelain Group.
Gwyn Hanssen
Pigott.** Porcelain.
Thrown. Max. height
18.5 cm (7 ¼ in).
1998

*Wood-fired so that
surfaces betray
small changes in
tonality where
the flame has
touched the pot,
this group shows
how Hanssen Pigott
is able to use a
great economy of
means to breath-
catching effect.*

◻ **Limoges
Porcelain Group.
Gwyn Hanssen
Pigott.** Porcelain.
Thrown. Max. height
9.5 cm (3 ¼ in).
1998

*These vessels
are as close to
the austerity of
laboratory retorts
and crucibles as
they are to pots for
domestic interiors.*

Still Life with Yellow Bowl. Gwyn Hanssen Pigott. Porcelain. Thrown. Max. height 27 cm (10¾ in). 1998

Using thrown porcelain vessels, Hanssen Pigott constructs groupings or still lives. They are reminiscent of the paintings of Morandi or Chardin, in which domestic pots are carefully considered and gain great symbolic significance through their placement.

Tie Box. Byron Temple. Stoneware. Thrown, cut feet. Salt glazed, wood-fired. 15 x 9 cm (6 x 3½ in). 1994

The lid of this box has been freely trimmed: a treatment that accords with the chance play of salt and wood fire on its surface. A linen thread adds to the slightly ritualistic feel that emanates from this piece.

Bamboo Jar. Byron Temple.
Stoneware. Thrown. Salt glazed, wood-fired. 12.5 x 12.5 cm (5 x 5 in). 1997

Softness of throwing and handling is contrasted with sharply turned planes to give this jar its austere character. Sealmarks, often hidden on pots, are used by Temple to understated decorative effect.

Porcelain Button Box. Byron Temple.
Stoneware. Thrown. Salt glazed, wood-fired.
.5 x 12 cm (3 x 4¾ in). 1996

This freedom of treatment with porcelain is refreshing: it is rarely used in this manner within studio ceramics.

(Untitled). Geert Lap.

Stoneware. Terra sigillata surface. Ø 42 cm
(16½ in). 1990

*Many potters are concerned with the profile
of their pots, particularly how they look in
photographs. Lap's skill, one that he shares
with the late Hans Coper, is to make pots
that have a sense of a real interior volume,
not just a fine silhouette.*

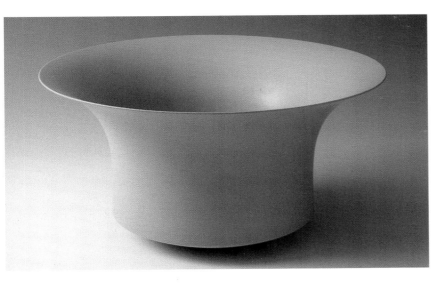

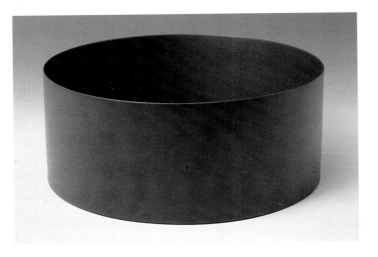

(Untitled). Geert Lap. Stoneware. Thrown. 14 x 23 cm (5½ x 9 in). 1987

This is a thrown form. But it is not concerned with the kinds of gesture that throwing usually makes: there are no overt lines left on the surface. Rather it has a surface that looks engineered in its purity, more metal than clay. The hidden foot gives it an exhilarating feeling of freedom from gravity.

(Untitled). Geert Lap. Stoneware. Thrown, terra sigillata surface. 24 x 32 cm (9½ x 12½ in). 1990

This is a play on the insubstantial. Again Lap creates a form that appears to float free of the earth, but it is also unclear whether it is a vessel, a bell or even a container at all. This kind of ambiguity makes Lap's works truly involving.

(Untitled). Geert Lap. Stoneware. Terra sigillata surface. Height 12.5 cm (5 in). 1990

A dish can be the most banal form possible. Lap seems to test the viewer as to the quality of their attention; will they allow the simplicity of this vessel to be contemplative or will they dismiss it out of hand? This is an Ur-pot - an elemental vessel - both basic and highly sophisticated.

◔ **Platter. Tsubusa Kato.**
Porcelain clay, celadon glaze.
Thrown. ∅ 30 cm (12 in).
1998

*This dish with its pooling
celadon glaze shows how Kato
enjoys playing off apparent
technical defects. Here the eye
is drawn in from the roughly
trimmed, torn edge of the dish
to the rich well of celadon in
the centre.*

◑ **Teacup. Tsubusa Kato.**
Porcelain clay, celadon glaze.
Thrown. Height 10 cm (4 in).
1998

*An unctuous celadon glaze
that is encouraged to run and
pool through over-firing gives
Kato's work its quality of
precariousness. Both porcelain
as a material and celadon as
a revered Oriental glaze are
rarely treated with this
energetic abandon.*

Bowls.
Annie Fourmanoir.
Porcelain. Thrown.
Max. height 11 cm
(4¼ in). 1996

*"Making something
simple out of
something difficult"
is how Fourmanoir
describes the way in
which she
approaches
porcelain. The
principle concern
behind these
deceptively austere
bowls is to create
forms that are
translucent and
finely balanced
without becoming
precious: this is
porcelain to be
used.*

Lipped Bowl.
Tsubusa Kato.
Porcelain clay,
celadon glaze.
Thrown. 11 x 25 cm
(4¼ x 9¾ in). 1998

*Kato is fond of the
ellipse created by
the severe warping
of round thrown
forms. His pots
often look as if they
are about to
collapse: indeed he
encourages and
utilizes the visual
tension between the
glaze qualities and
the cracking and
slumping that can
occur in firing.*

 **Oval Teapots. Julian Stair.** Porcelain with wisteria handle. Thrown and constructed. Max. height 23 cm (9 in). 1998

These oval teapots have been constructed in complex ways but still retain the energy of their thrown components. The handles have been woven from wisteria fronds and the open and relaxed manner of their making contrasts pleasingly with that of the pots.

Oval Dish. Julian Stair. Porcelain. Thrown and constructed. 31 x 28 cm (12¼ x 11 in). 1998

Constructing forms from porcelain is notoriously difficult, with the possibility of cracking always present. The success of this dish lies in the dynamic movement of the intersecting lines, picked up by the clear white glaze.

Teacaddy. Julian Stair.
Red stoneware. Thrown and constructed.
⌀ 29 cm (11½ in). 1998

Teacaddies by name only, Stair's constructed boxes look towards the symbolic functions of casket or funerary wares as much as to the more overtly domestic uses.

Porcelain Jugs. Julian Stair. Thrown and facetted. Semi-matt glaze. Max. height 17 cm (6¾ in). 1998

Stair makes deep facets into pots that he has just thrown, while they are still damp on the wheel: this gives them immediacy.

**Pair of Oval Dishes.
Prue Venables.**
Porcelain. Hand-thrown and altered.
15 x 11 x 10.5 cm
(6 x 4¼ x 4 in). 1996

Venables throws her forms without bases, bending them into shape while still flexible. They are then constructed with slabbed bases and slowly dried.

**Teapot and Cup.
Prue Venables.**
Porcelain. Hand-thrown and altered.
Left: 9.5 x 9 x 6 cm
(3¾ x 3½ x 2¼ in).
Right: 19 x 14 x
8.5 cm (7½ x 5½ x
3¼ in). 1995

Attenuated to an almost mannered degree, this cup and teapot have an air of grandeur about them.

Bottle and Oval Bowl. Prue Venables.
Porcelain. Hand-thrown and altered.
Left: 18.7 x 10 x 7 cm (7½ x 4 x 2¾ in). Right: 8 x 25 cm (3 x 9¾ in). 1997

Gentle distortion, as in these vessels, makes the tension between volume and profile more intriguing. The eye works to understand how deep and round the vessels are.

Yellow Bowl and Jug. Prue Venables.
Porcelain. Hand-thrown and altered.
Left: 8.4 x 18.3 cm (3¼ x 7 in). Right: 12 x 8.3 x 4.5 cm (4¾ x 3¼ x 1¾ in). 1997

This colour of glaze has a luminosity heightened by the clarity of the edges of the forms. The form of the jug cleverly edits out the paraphernalia we associate with a pouring vessel: all that is left is the gentle modulation of the rim.

Teapot. Rob Barnard. Stoneware, naturally occurring ash glaze. Anagama-fired. 22 x 17 cm (8¾ x 6¾ in). 1997

This is a generous teapot, broadly and confidently thrown. All Barnard's pots are meant to be used: here the texture of the handle has a pleasing roughness.

Vase. Rob Barnard. Stoneware, naturally occurring ash glaze. Anagama-fired. 24 x 16 cm (9½ x 6¼ in). 1997

In a long wood firing ash can settle on the shoulders of pots, forming a natural glaze as here, where rivulets of ash have fallen away from the shoulder and pooled in the inscribed lines. The sense of flux and of unpredictability in the kiln has been much prized in Japanese ceramics, and is often compared to the way in which lichen and moss gather on stone.

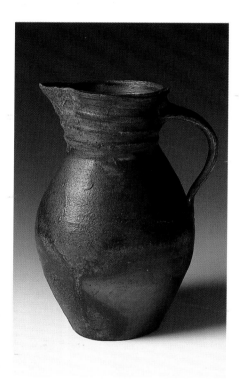

Pitcher. Rob Barnard. Stoneware, naturally occurring ash glaze. Anagama-fired. 24 x 18 cm (9½ x 7 in). 1997

This pitcher is a fusion of a Western form, common since medieval times, with a Japanese aesthetic. Here is a pot that exemplifies pleasure derived from its making and firing: the free throwing marks have been left to give a sense of the energy that went into the process.

Vase. Rob Barnard. Stoneware, naturally occurring ash glaze. Anagama-fired. 23 x 10 cm (9 x 4 in). 1997

Using strong throwing rings, Barnard created an interesting surface on which the subtle variations of the firing can play.

ARCHITECTURAL FORM

Pots, like buildings, are containers. In the long and involved history

of ceramics, this conjunction has often been explored: T'ang

Dynasty Chinese houses, sheepfolds and towers or the elaborate

terracotta fantasies made to sit on the roofs of French farmhouses

are cases in point. Constructed ceramics

have often looked to architectural form: to

the planes and edges, interstices, corners,

openings and curves that make up the

external surfaces of buildings. Clay slabs can be cut, facetted,

ground down or polished to create textures and shadows that

resonate with buildings: Martin Smith has made works that are

direct responses to Italian Renaissance structures. But the interior

space of vessels can also echo enclosed architectural space. From

funerary urns to teacaddies, ceramics have been made and are

being made that respond to architecture. The inner life of

architectural form is a rich metaphor for ceramics.

Black Pierced Form. David Binns.
Grogged clay, copper oxide, manganese
dioxide and vanadium pentoxide. Pierced and
shaped in fabric former, fired to 1100°C.
48 x 48 cm (19 x 19 in). 1997

*Binns is fascinated by mathematical patterns.
His work plays with ideas of repetition and
rhythm, creating ceramic pieces that are
suggestive of scientific structures.*

Sgraffito Vessel. Masimichi Yoshikawa.
Porcelain, thrown and slab-built. Cobalt-
compound slip, iron silicate celadon glaze.
28 x 26.5 x 38 cm (11 x 10½ x 15 in). 1997

*Cobalt decoration is used to emphasize
the gestural nature of these vessels; it looks
as though previous pretty designs have
been crossed out by these strong, grafitti-
like markings.*

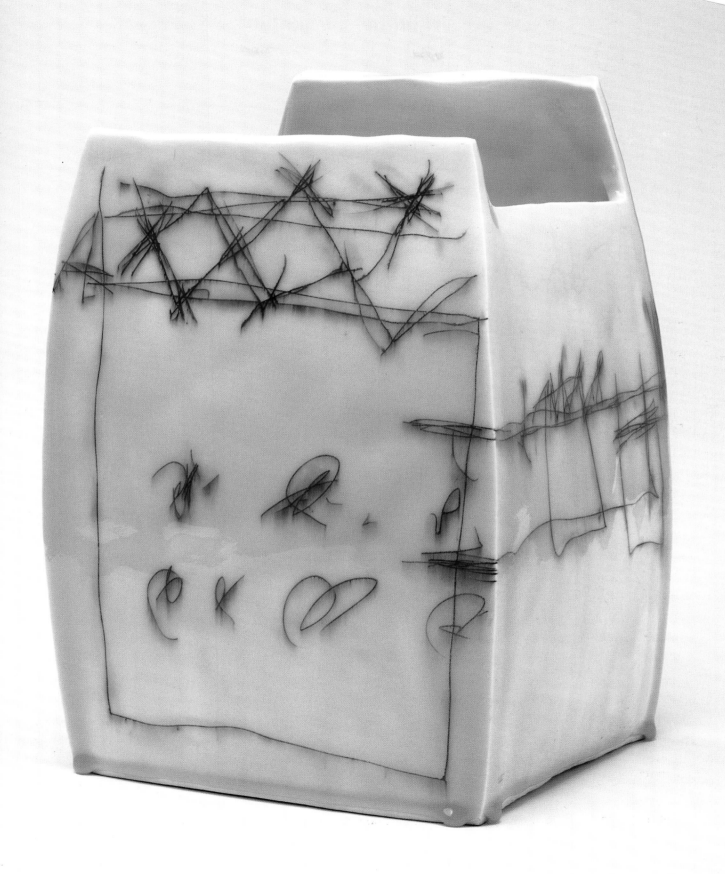

Nikko Traverse. Roberta Griffith. Low-fired, white clay. Hand-built. 9 x 18 x 18 cm (3½ x 11 x 11 in). 1994

Nikko is a seventeenth-century Japanese shrine, a multi-coloured mix of buildings, statues and scarlet-lacquered arches. Both this and "Nikko Transfer" (opposite) have echoes of the architecture. In this piece, geometric lines are displaced by a disruptive traverse section: the eye does not know where to settle.

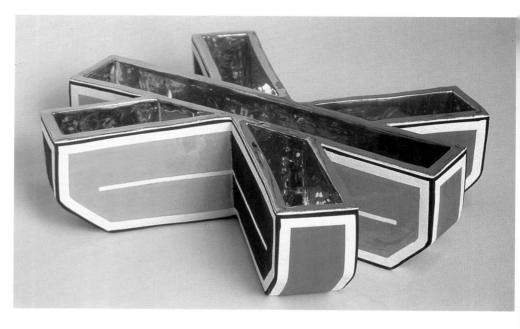

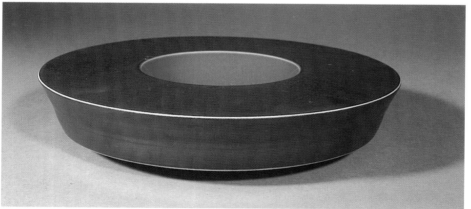

Vessel. Thomas Bohle. Stoneware, celadon glaze. Raw and celadon glazed, double-walled, reduction-fired. 16.5 x 17 cm (6½ x 6¾ in). 1996

This double-walled piece looks as if it has been turned on a lathe – with a profile that is suggestive of architectural or industrial processes rather than craft. It is a piece made with remarkable clarity; undemonstrative yet impressive.

Bowl. Thomas Bohle. Stoneware, oxblood/copper red glaze, feldspatic glaze. Double-walled, reduction-fired. 6 x 33 cm (2¼ x 13 in). 1997

Bohle uses a throwing technique that allows for double walls, creating a vessel that has two distinct internal chambers. This can be exploited to create mystifying disparities between internal volume and external profile. Here he creates an elegantly wide disc bowl that seems weightless because of its hidden foot.

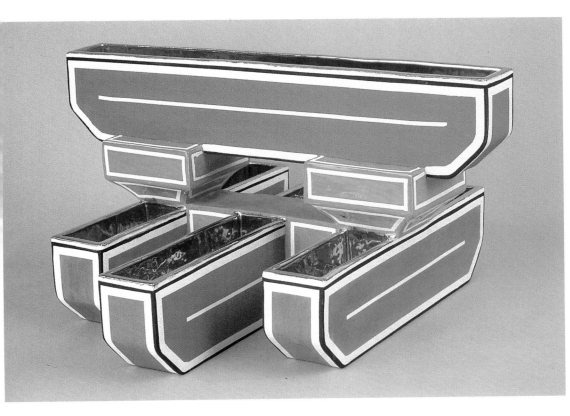

⬡ **Nikko Transfer. Roberta Griffith.** Low-fired, white clay. Hand-built. 8.5 x 38.5 x 38.5 cm (3¼ x 15¼ x 15¼ in). 1994

This is a witty take on a ceremonial Japanese arch. Part building, part catamaran, this hand-built piece is a complex of disparate geometry that defies the onlooker to interpret it.

⬡ **Vessel. Thomas Bohle.** Stoneware, ox blood/copper red glaze. Double-walled, reduction-fired. 16 x 20 cm (6¼ x 8 in). 1996

The rich red glaze has pulled away from below the rim leaving a graphic point of punctuation. This unctuous glaze, with its historical resonances of Imperial Chinese ceramics, is used here on a form of modernist clarity.

ARCHITECTURAL FORM

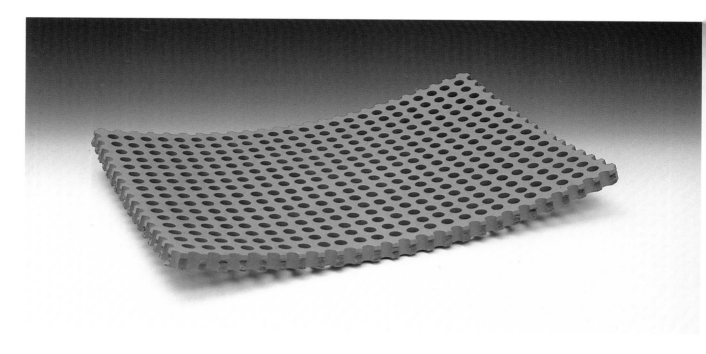

⬡ **Terracotta Pierced Form. David Binns.** Terracotta clay. Fired to 1100°C, ground and polished after firing. 48 X 38 cm (19 X 15 in). 1996

This piece manages to present itself as both a ruthless investigation into geometric pattern and an almost lyrical fragment broken from some larger, lost structure. Terracotta, with its deep resonances of buildings, tiles and brick, is a fertile material for sculptural ceramics.

▽ **White Pierced Form. David Binns.** Heavily grogged white clay. Slab-built, pierced and shaped in fabric former, fired to 1100°C, ground and polished after firing. 74 x 20 cm (29½ x 8 in). 1996

This piece holds two opposing processes in tension; the strong punctuating of the form and the fine polishing of the surface.

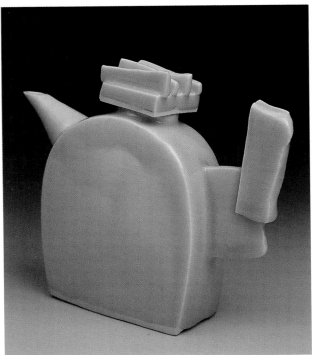

◯ **Teapot.**
Masimichi Yoshikawa.
Porcelain, celadon
glaze. Thrown and slab-
built. 18 x 6.5 x 19 cm
(7 x 2½ x 7½ in). 1995

*Porcelain is often
used tentatively and
preciously. Here it is
used with gusto: the
thick slabs convey
an impression of
energetic handling
in construction.*

◯ **Teapot with Two Spouts and Teabowls.**
Masimichi Yoshikawa. Porcelain, Imari-style
celadon glaze. Thrown and slab-built.
Teapot: 23 x 10 x 25 cm (9 x 4 x 9¾ in).
Teabowls: 7 x 7 x 8 cm (2¾ x 2¾ x 3⅛ in).
1997

*If pots and buildings do come together, then
this is a ceramic folly. It is a piece of joie-de-
vivre, a two-spouted, multi-footed porcelain
teapot. It manages to be both vaguely
anthropomorphic with its two outstretched
arms, and yet unsettling.*

Seen and Unseen No. 1. Martin Smith.
Red earthenware, platinum leaf. Press-moulded. 15 x 45 cm (6 x 17¾ in). 1995

Deep cuts made with a double-bladed diamond saw cross the base of this piece. Unlike other "grounded" vessels, Smith explores the ambiguity of not knowing where a base ends.

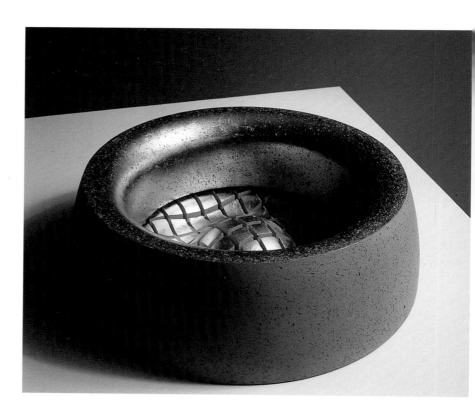

Two Bowl Forms. Martin Smith. Red earthenware. Jigger and jolleyed sections, cut and assembled. Left: cut interior painted white. Length 33.9 cm (13½ in). 1985 Right: ochre interior with blue diamond pattern. Width 32 cm (12½ in).

Smith has been much influenced by Renaissance architecture, as in these pieces which are reminiscent of the marble floors of stone churches. The techniques that Smith employs of routing, polishing, sawing and grinding are more akin to a stonemason's than a potter's.

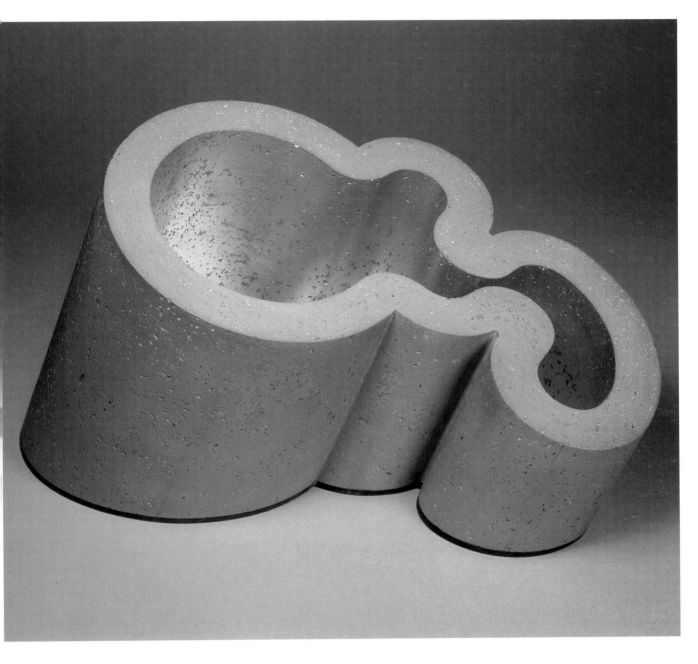

Curved Vessel. Martin Smith. Red brick clay, slate, gold leaf. Press-moulded.
28.5 cm (11½ in) wide. 1992

There are radically different densities in the three materials used in this piece,
red clay for the body of the form, slate for the base and gold leaf for the interior.
It has been press-moulded in two parts, with the interior formed by means of a
sliding template.

Invention.
Ken Eastman. White
stoneware clay, coloured
slips and oxides. Slab-
built and painted, fired
several times at 1180°C.
17 x 15.5 x 17 cm
(6¾ x 6¼ x 6¾ in).
1997

*Eastman often
juxtaposes diverse
volumes and shapes,
like a child's building
blocks, challenging us
to make sense of the
outcome.*

Form and Content. Ken Eastman.
White stoneware clay, coloured slips and
oxides. Slab-built and painted, fired several
times at 1180°C. 30 x 18 x 60 cm
(12 x 7 x 24 in). 1997

*Do these works fit together, should one
contain the other? They seem to be too
simple, almost an exercise in construction,
and so become curiously unsettling.*

Still Life. Ken Eastman. White stoneware
clay, coloured slips and oxides. Slab-built and
painted, fired several times at 1180°C.
18 x 18 x 40 cm (7 x 7 x 16 in). 1997

*The surfaces of Eastman's work have a
luminosity acquired through being painted with
vitreous slips and given multiple firings. This
gives them the magical ability to look both
evanescent and remarkably dense.*

This complex interlocking piece is a matrix of planes, interstices and shadows. It has the grandeur of a city scape, far beyond its scale.

◖ **Cut-outs (detail). Ken Eastman.** White stoneware clay, coloured slips and oxides. Slab-built and painted, fired several times at 1180°C. 16 x 16 x 16 cm (6¼ x 6¼ x 6¼ in) each. 1998

This play with inverse and obverse shadows echoes the workbench, the geometry lesson and the pastry cook. Perhaps they are working drawings in clay for an architect.

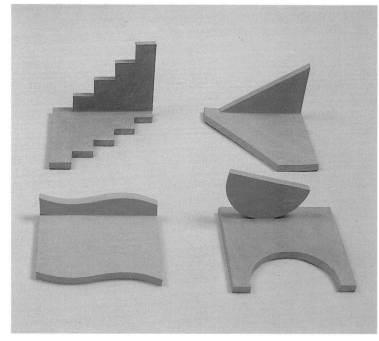

◖ **Shelf Life. Ken Eastman.** White stoneware clay, coloured slips and oxides. Slab-built and painted, fired several times at 1180°C. 20 x 20 x 160 cm (8 x 8 x 63½ in). 1995

"Left on the Shelf", "shelved": this piece is a punning grouping of six disparate forms, carefully placed in a row. This conjunction of forms seems to contain a contradictory rationale.

43

ARCHITECTURAL FORM

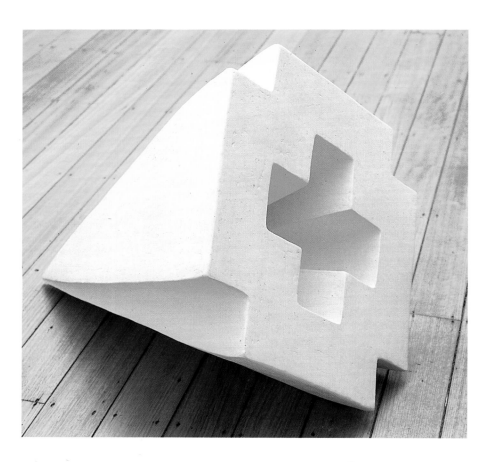

🔺 **Halved. Pilar Rojas.** Ceramic. Coiled walls supported by clay brackets, burnished earthenware slips, fired at 1050°C. 65 x 70 x 65 cm (25½ x 27½ x 25½ in). 1997

Mould, outer casing or abandoned armature, "Halved" is an ambiguous work. Its construction, hard edged and definite, suggests a lost architectural function.

🔻 **Elements. Pilar Rojas.** Earthenware. Hand-built, burnished, fired at 1050°C. Approx. 15 x 10 x 5 cm (6 x 4 x 2 in) each. 1996-1997

Rojas is intrigued by coded meanings, and many of her works play with language. In this series, the elemental objects look as if they have wandered from a chemistry laboratory.

(Untitled). Ruth Duckworth. Porcelain.
12 x 13.5 cm (4¾ x 5¼ in). 1995

Duckworth has consistently pioneered new areas of sculptural ceramics. This interlocking piece has the gravitas of ancient Cycladic sculpture.

(Untitled). Ruth Duckworth.
Porcelain. 16.5 x 24 cm (6½ x 9½ in).
1990

Perfectly poised, this balancing work is resonant with abstracted natural imagery. It has a strength that comes from Duckworth's fine definition of attenuated planes and full volumes.

RETHINKING THE FIGURE

FIGURATION REFLECTS HOW A CULTURE understands and values the body. Contemporary ceramics that take the body as their theme are often unsettling rather than contemplative: these are bodies that are part of our complex modernity, not symbols of perfection. Broken up, patched, fragmentary, collaged or even camouflaged, they suggest that we experience the world in diverse ways, through different thoughts and emotions. The most radical pieces may be a commentary on historical ceramics, or on issues of gender.

A Bevy of Masterful Cock-Queens. **Grayson Perry.** Earthenware. Slip, gold lustre on sprigs, copper and cobalt oxide painting, photographic transfers. Height 33 cm (13 in). 1996

The images on Perry's pots show how politicized figuration has become. These images are not the safe stereotypical views of sexuality and gender.

Dancer. **Michael Flynn.** Ceramic. Hand-built, raku. Height 45 cm (18 in). 1997

Where Dresden or Meissen Commedia dell'Arte figures are poised and polite in their stated activities and role-playing, Flynn's have a wild, subversive quality. His "Dancer" is almost Bacchic in its abandon.

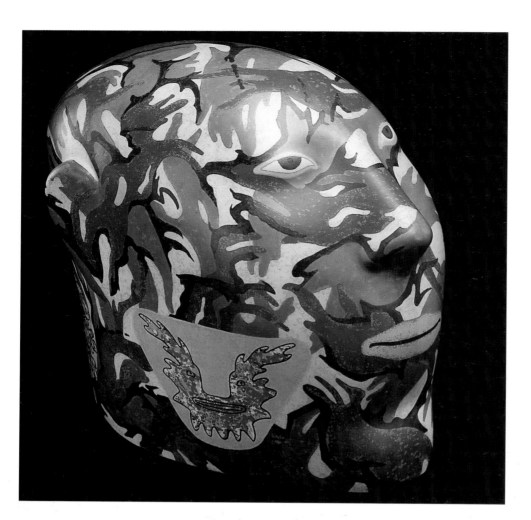

Green Man. Tony Bennett.
Earthenware and stains. Coloured slip painted into mould and cast, fired once and burnished. Height 33 cm (13 in). 1997

Camouflage can break up the profile of forms and conceal: here it is vivid and eye-catching. This head, with its British Army camouflage livery, is that of a "modern warrior", protector of wildlife.

Urban Camouflage. Tony Bennett. Earthenware. Press-moulded and slip-cast, white earthenware slip, coloured slips, earthenware glazes. Height 41 cm (16 in). 1997

The head is powerful and buttress-like, with a slightly Art Deco feel to it.

48

Urban Camouflage (detail). Tony Bennett.

These surfaces have been moulded from found objects, such as car mats, Lego and corrugated cardboard.

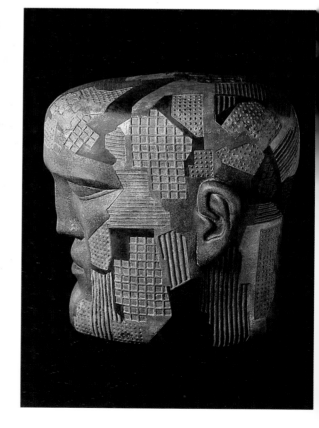

◀ **Figure. Mo Jupp.** Earthenware. Hand-built. Height 47 cm (18½ in). 1998

Impossibly attenuated, Jupp's figures have the condensed irreducible energy of rapid sketches with clay. Jupp's way of using clay in a collage-like manner adds to this sense.

△ **Portrait of J. Mo Jupp.** Slab-built. High-fired red earthenware pedestal and high fired stoneware foot. 12 x 8 x 25 cm (4¾ x 3¼ x 9¾ in). 1998

This foot, proudly stranded on its grand plinth, comes from a series of portraits of women's feet. It has both classical delusions (a fragment of antiquity) and the pathos of a single lost shoe.

◆ **Carolus Rex. Stephen Dixon.** Ceramic (s.t. material clay, earthenware, lead glaze). Slab-built, modelled, decorated with sprigs, monoprints, coloured slips, glazes, enamels and lustres. 36 x 42 x 19 cm (14 x 16 x 7 in). 1997

A scabrous portrait of the future King Charles, as a Don Quixote figure, looking for a role. He carries his head in his hands in the posture of a martyred saint.

◆ **Sunflowers + Spice Girls.**
Stephen Dixon. Ceramic (s.t. material clay, earthenware, lead glaze at fired at 1120°C). Slab-built, decorated with stamps, monoprints, coloured slips, glazes, enamels and lustres. 22 x 36 x 19 cm (9 x 14 x 7 in). 1997

Dixon's simple fluid forms contrast with the welter of diverse decorative techniques. There is a feeling of a collage of ideas and impressions; Van Gogh's "Sunflowers" and the Spice Girls sit shoulder to shoulder in this excoriating work.

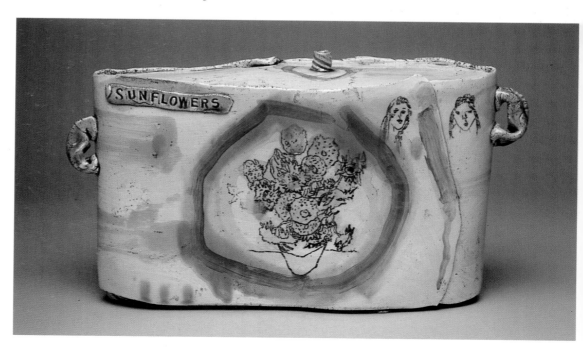

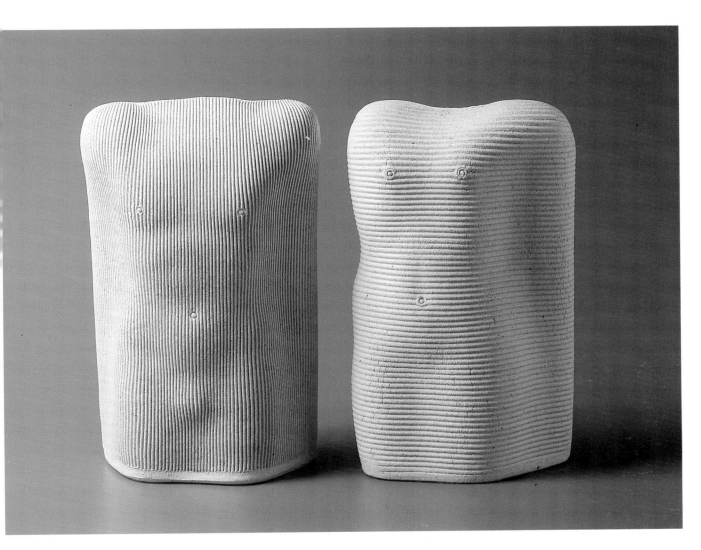

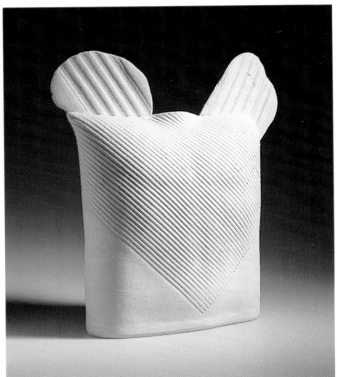

◑ **Family of Angels, 2.**
Vladimir Tsivin. China clay and
grog. Height 38 cm (15 in).
1990

*Vestigial wings turn this torso
into an iconic angle. Tsivin
works with a pared-down
technique to make these quiet
ceramic monuments.*

◭ **Man and Woman.**
Vladimir Tsivin. Porcelain and
chamotte with touches of glaze.
Left: 36 x 19.5 cm (14¼ x 7½ in).
Right: 35.3 x 19cm (14 x 7½ in).
1989

*Made from impressed slabs of clay
that are gently distorted, these
torsos have the peaceful energy of
archaic fragments; more
powerfully suggestive than full
figures would be.*

Man and Woman. Geoffrey Fuller. Earthenware. Slab-built, moulds, coloured slips with earthenware pigment, bisilicate glazes. Height 56 cm (22 in). 1997

Man, woman, tree and star: Fuller uses a simple grouping that has archetypal associations. Almost affected in its stylizing of features and proportions, it still manages to convey a real affection for its subject.

Greyhound. Geoffrey Fuller. Earthenware. Slab clay moulded base, coloured slips with earthenware pigment, lead bisilicate glaze. Height 30 cm (12 in). 1995

Fuller employs lead glazes on earthenware to give his work the tonal quality found in eighteenth-century Staffordshire figurines. This dog is the embodiment of suppressed energy.

Hobby Horse. Geoffrey Fuller. Earthenware. Slab clay, coloured slips with earthenware pigments, lead bisilicate glaze. Height 36 cm (14 in). 1997

This peculiar, almost totemic, fusion of man and beast is inspired by the creatures found in folk tales and Morris dances.

**"Drummer" from Monkey Band.
Michael Flynn.** Stoneware. Hand-built. Height 20 cm (8 in). 1997

Flynn revisits an eighteenth-century conceit, the animal orchestra, and gives it a powerful new interpretation. His impasto handling of clay is exemplary in its immediacy.

**To Catch a Cock II.
Michael Flynn.** Ceramic. Hand-built, raku. Height 40 cm (16 in). 1997

The symbolism of the cockerel, vain and sexually arrogant, but also vigilant and necessary, is both pagan and Christian. Here are two bundles of highly sexualized energy in full flight.

Figures from the series: The Cast of Characters (detail). Christie Brown.
Ceramic. Press-moulded. 1995

54

Clone I. Christie Brown. Ceramic.
Press-moulded. 74 x 35 x 18 cm
(29½ x 13¾ x 7 in). 1995

Archaic Greek kouroi *provide the inspiration for many of these figures. As with much modern art of the early twentieth century, the use of the archaic or totemic has been of great significance.*

Child of Glass 3. Christie Brown.
Ceramic. Press-moulded. 73 x 25 x 15 cm
(28¾ x 9¾ x 6 in). 1995

*These are not seamless bodies of perfection.
Brown's technique of construction involves
the use of quantities of layered press-
moulded sections, enabling her to give the
figures an impression of vulnerability.*

**Figures from the series: The Cast of
Characters. Christie Brown.** Ceramic. Press-
moulded. Max. height 75 cm (30 in). 1995

*Modern psychology has been a profound
influence on Brown. Her figures adopt roles,
or have multiple personalities that are far
from the norm.*

Style. Richard Slee.
Earthenware. Hand-built, glazed, underglaze transfer print, gold lustre. Height 50 cm (20 in). 1997

Literally a stile, metaphorically a take on Baroque style itself, this piece exemplifies Slee's way of condensing historical ceramic references and contemporary kitsch.

Boy in Field. Richard Slee. Earthenware, found figure, epoxy resin. Hand-built, glazed. Length 43 cm (17 in). 1997

Slee employs found figurines frequently in his work. Here a pastiche eighteenth-century figurine is given a landscape to gaze on. It manages to convey great humour and pathos simultaneously.

Boy in Field (detail). Richard Slee.

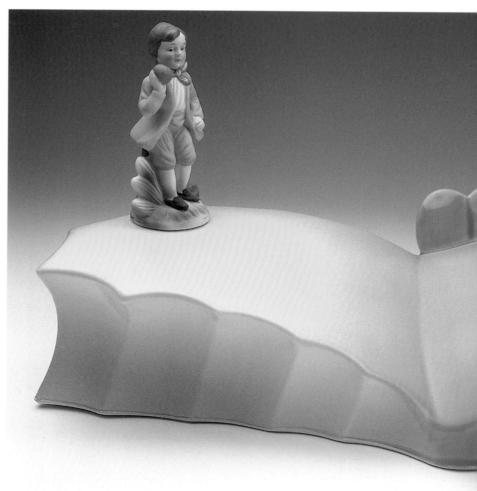

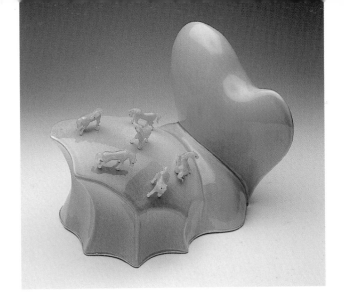

Landscape with Horses. Richard Slee.
Earthenware, found figures (glass), epoxy resin.
Hand-built, glazed. Height 29 cm (11½ in). 1997

*Glass figurines of horses are scattered on this
Elysian field with a cartoon hill rising behind
them. These are colours that come from
American comics or from the perfect versions of
history found in reproduction ceramics.*

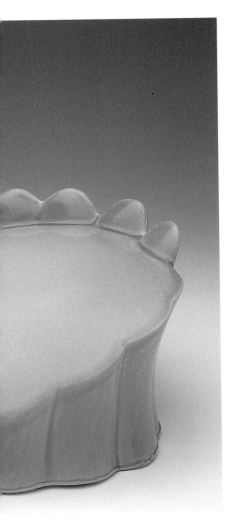

Jar. Richard Slee. Earthenware, found
ceramic figures, epoxy resin. Hand-built, glazed.
Height 50 cm (20 in). 1997

*Four found pastoral figures deck the corners of
this lidded jar. It is a baroque confection of
curves and swelling form, acting as an ironic
stand for these hapless figures.*

Two Children Born on the Same Day. Grayson Perry. Earthenware. Coiled, earthenware sprigs, graffito, copper oxide, gold lustre and photographic transfers. Height 36 cm (14 in). 1996

The most conventional of urn shapes, redolent of associations with formal Victorian pottery, is subverted by the cacophony of competing imagery and colours.

58

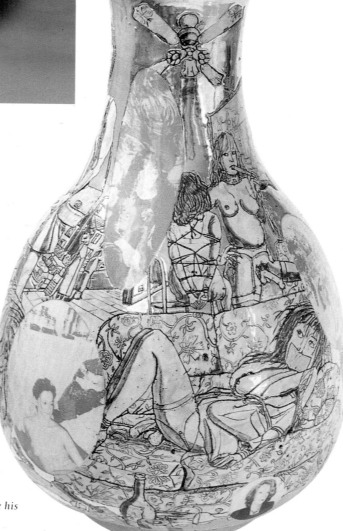

Bad Art Bad Pottery. Grayson Perry. Earthenware. Coiled, marbled and stencilled slip, graffito and manganese oxide, gold lustre and photographic transfers. Height 56 cm (22 in). 1996

Semi-clad figures decorating Victorian "High Art Pottery" were extremely conventional, depicting classical scenes in passive, codified ways. Perry revisits this kind of vessel, but here his figures are self-consciously and actively sexualized.

**Sex, Drugs and Earthenware.
Grayson Perry.** Earthenware.
Coiled, stencilled slip, sprigs and
gold lustre, cobalt oxide painting,
impressed text, open stock and
photographic transfers. Height
64 cm (25 in). 1995

*Earthenware is not the
usual home for such happily
transgressive activities.*

**I Saw This Vase and Thought It
Beautiful Then I Looked At It
(detail). Grayson Perry.**
Earthenware. Stencilled slip,
graffito, copper oxide, photographic
transfers. Height 50 cm (20 in).
1995

*Layered stencils and transfers
produce a complex surface of
suggestion, imagery and
commentary. The title could stand
for the double-take quality of any
of Perry's works.*

59

RETHINKING THE FIGURE

ELEMENTAL
FORMS

GIVEN THAT CERAMICS USES THE FOUR ELEMENTS of fire, earth, air and water, it is unsurprising that there has always been a strand of potters who are concerned with the elemental. Given that the metamorphic process that turns earth into fired clay and turns minerals into glazes is one of powerful dynamism, it is clear that ceramicists can use the imagery of this process in their work. Enlivening and complex, a matrix of the found and the made, the new, the aged and the broken, these are not earthbound pots.

The Roman Collection XI. Irene Vonck.
Stoneware, engobe, pigments. Fired to 1160°C.
25 x 25 x 21 cm (9¾ x 9¾ x 8¼ in). 1998

Part of the appeal of Vonck's work is that it enacts the tension between order and chaos, each piece retains the unformed material in juxtaposition with the formed vessel.

Monumental Jar. Claudi Casanovas.
Mixed media stoneware.

Casanovas is amongst the most ambitious of makers using clay. This jar seems to speak both the language of vessels – it is like an oil or grain jar from an earlier culture – and that of geological process. It seems both made and found simultaneously.

◭ **(Untitled). Sara Radstone.** Slab-built,
oxidized stoneware. Height 20 - 21 cm
(8 - 8¼ in). 1997

▽ **Little Volumes. Sara Radstone.**
Slab-built stoneware. Height 8 - 10 cm
(3 - 4 in). 1997

◐ ◑ **(Untitled Pair).**
Sara Radstone. Slab-built,
oxidized stoneware. Height
152 cm and 166 cm
(59¾ in and 65¼ in). 1994-95

*Radstone came to prominence
in the 1980s with a sequence
of strange and ambiguous
vessels, often with only the
most vestigial of openings to
suggest that they were
containers.*

*With their painstakingly
textured and eroded surfaces,
they bridged ideas of
vulnerability and permanence.
They seemed to be close to
both weathered natural objects
and to the scarred, discarded
detritus of human life – paper
bags or old clothes.*

*With these pieces, Radstone
is still treading this sensitive
line, but they have become
closer to archeological objects,
strange fragments from
forgotten rituals. They have
the sense of an organic form
that has been much used, like
an old flint tool, or the
wooden haft of an axe.*

ELEMENTAL FORMS

▷ **Wadi, Negev Desert. Jenny Beavan.** T material, coloured slips and engobes, glazes and indigenous materials. Assembled from slabs of rock impressions. 30 x 55 x 49 cm (12 x 21½ x 19½ in). 1997

Beavan's work is haunted by the dynamic process of geological change – the decay, disintegration and reformation that creates landscape. This piece was assembled from slabs made by rock impressions.

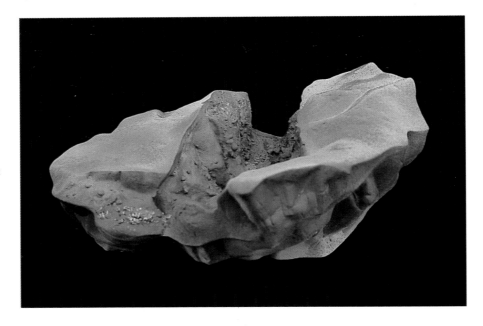

▽ **Geo-Vector, Rock Formation in Thin Section. Jenny Beavan.** Porcelain with molochite, river mud, coloured slips and found materials. Slab-built. 29 x 52 x 32 cm (11½ x 20½ x 12½ in). 1998

Found materials, including river mud, beach sands and mining waste, build up the complex surface of these vessels. This use of the indigenous is a response to the particularity of place.

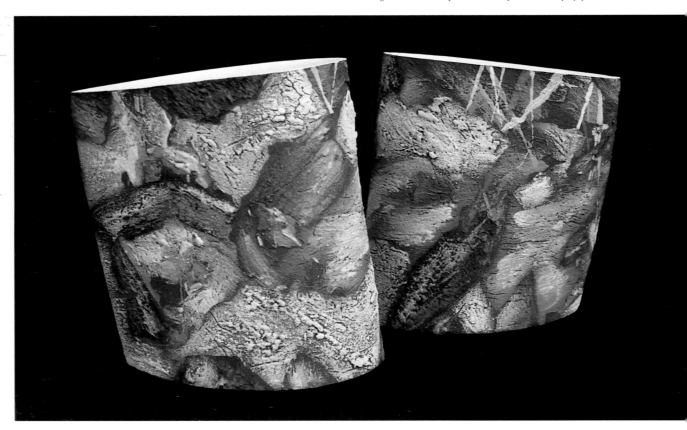

The Roman Collection XII. Irene Vonck.
Stoneware, engobe, pigments. Made in two parts: manipulated, solid clay, and coil-built, 1160°C firing. 25 x 23 x 26 cm (9¾ x 9 x 10¼ in). 1998

Inspired by the changing character of rocks lying half-submerged in an Andean river, Vonck's work contrasts a material affected by shaping and one in its natural state.

The Roman Collection V. Irene Vonck.
Stoneware, engobe, pigments. Form made in two parts: manipulated, solid clay and coil-built, 1160°C firing. 25 x 15 x 27 cm (9¾ x 6 x 10¾ in). 1998

The soft flowing lines of the vessel element of this piece act as a metaphor for the eroding powers of water. The success of this work is that it is not about literal equations between natural and human forces, but about suggestion and possibility.

The Curaçao Collection no. 50. Irene Vonck.
Stoneware, engobe, pigments. Coil-built, 1160°C firing. 30 x 40 x 24 cm (12 x 16 x 9½ in). 1997

This series of seductive volumes invokes the strangeness of natural underwater forms. The ambiguity of these subterranean forms lies in the fact that they are lived-in vessels.

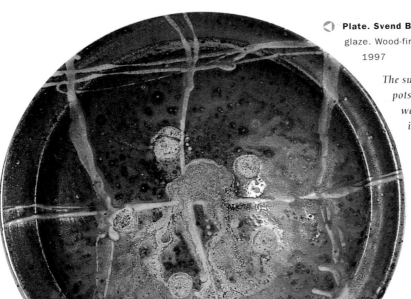

Plate. Svend Bayer. Stoneware clay, shino glaze. Wood-fired. 13 x 56 cm (5 x 22 in). 1997

The subdued colouring of wood-fired pots is often compared to that of weathered rock or timber, an image that resonates with this plate. Bayer creates a loose grid with a trailed glaze that gives a structure for the random marks to work against.

Vase with Shells. Svend Bayer. Stoneware clay. Wood-fired. 56 x 56 cm (22 x 22 in). 1997

This pot was fired on its side, resting on scallop shells. For much of the four-day firing it would have been covered in embers which eventually melted, forming an ash glaze. It looks like a survivor from some elemental process.

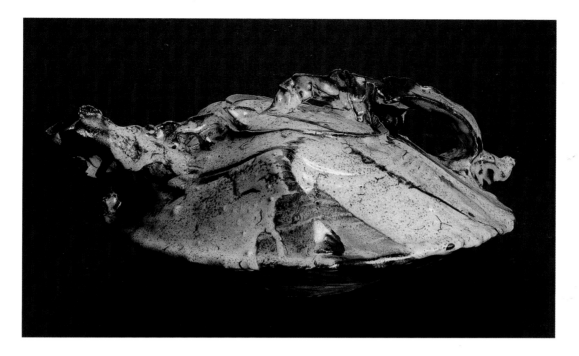

Teapot. **Claude Champy.** Stoneware. Wood-fired, two glazes. 18 x 38 cm (7 x 15 in). 1997

A teapot form, but one that has been subject not to the rigours of functional requirements, but to broad decorative treatment.

Before Ankorage. **Claude Champy.** Stoneware. Wood-fired to cone 9-10, two glazes. 70 x 70 cm (28 x 28 in). 1990

This piece is less a functional form than a comment on the process of wood-firing that turns a malleable material into one that is exactingly hard.

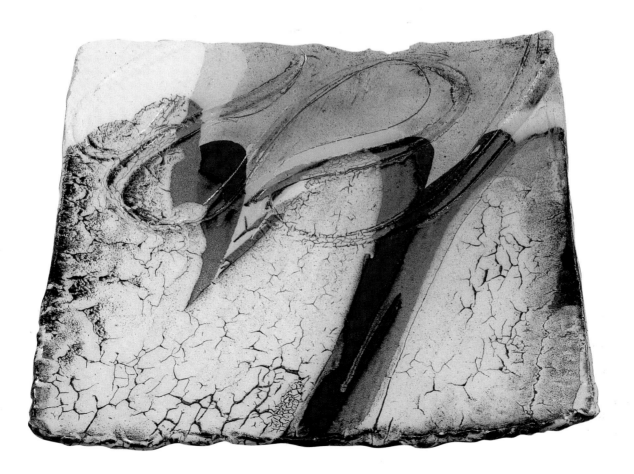

Large Dish. Claudi Casanovas.
Mixed media stoneware. Hand-built.
⌀ 145 cm (57½ in). 1991

*Casanovas' huge dishes push his
use of clay into another dimension.
The scale is such that you cannot
comprehend it by touch, but need to
walk round it.*

Teabowl. Claudi Casanovas. Mixed media
stoneware. Thrown. ⌀ 13 cm (5¼ in). 1996

*Casanovas uses the teabowl form as a way
of exploring structure. His "deconstructed"
forms echo the bones and lineaments of
vessels, such as the timbers of a boat.*

◁ ◯ **Teabowls.**
Claudi Casanovas. Mixed
media stoneware. Thrown.
Top: ⌀ 15 cm (6 in). 1996.
Bottom: ⌀ 19 cm (7 ½ in).
1996

*These teabowls are visually
close to the burrs and knots
of wood: there is a sense of
frozen time, of ageing made
visible. Teabowls are usually
objects of solace and
contemplation, fitting into
cupped hands, but these
wayward forms are more
akin to gesticulating hands
than to the meditative norms.*

▽ (Left) **No1/Green Scroll.**
Gillian Lowndes. Porcelain, slip-dipped fibre glass. 11.5 x 30.5 cm (4½ x 12 in). 1997

▽ (Right) **White Scroll, Objects of Our Time.**
Gillian Lowndes. Bone china, slip-dipped fibre glass. 13 x 31 cm (5¼ x 12¼ in). 1997

Lowndes' scroll pieces may seem to have only the most distant relationship with ceramics. Indeed, until touched, their resemblance lies with bales of paper or scrapyard metal. However, their worn and archaic surfaces attest to ceramic processes.

 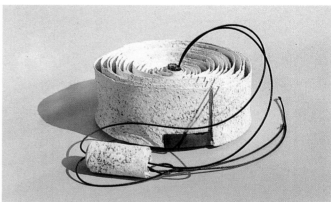

◁ **Two "Constructs".**
Gillian Lowndes. Porcelain, slip-dipped fibre glass, sieve, wire. Max. height 150 cm (59 in). 1998

▷ **Small Wall Scrolls.**
Gillian Lowndes. Porcelain, slip-dipped fibre glass, forks. Max. height 64 cm (25¼ in). 1998

These are three-dimensional collages. Constructed after firing from small utensils and ceramic elements, they have an almost totemic feel of known, domestic items transfigured into objects of otherness. Broken in parts with distressed edges, they carry an elemental charge with them.

Landform Series. Alison Brown. White stoneware clay, earthenware glazes. Thrown, carved and reassembled. 22 x 24 cm (8¾ x 9½ in). Bowl ⌀ 20 cm (8 in). 1995

With its tripod feet and vestigial carved handle, this vessel plays with ideas of ritual.

Landform Series. Alison Brown. White stoneware clay, dry glaze and lustre. Thrown and altered, carved and reassembled, high fired bisque (1200°C), fired glaze (1040°C), post glaze lustre (850°C). 10 x 14 cm (4 x 5½ in). 1996

Inspired by the dramatic geography of Australia, this thrown and carved bowl makes connections between geological shifts and the movement made in throwing.

Spirit and Place. Alison Brown. White stoneware clay, oxides and underglaze pigment. Slab form, fired to 1150°C, 8-10 layered and scraped colours. 40 x 65 x 15 cm (16 x 26 x 6 in). 1996

Multiple layers of colour from oxides and pigments were scraped back to give the depth of surface on this piece. Inspired by a photograph of a shadow in the landscape, it is strongly atmospheric of the temporal and the insubstantial.

◐ **Oval Mouth Vessel. Jeff Shapiro.** Ceramic.
Thrown and altered, anagama-fired.
30 x 27 x 14 cm (12 x 10½ x 5½ in). 1997

*Distorting this severe, upright bowl form into
an oval gives it a strong sense of displacement.
With any distorted shape, the eye makes a play
with how it must have been originally.*

▷ **Vessel with Shell No. 2. Jeff Shapiro.**
Carved from solid clay, anagama-fired.
14 x 12.5 x 12.5 cm (5½ x 5 x 5 in). 1996

*Shapiro is one of a generation of American
potters to use Japanese wood-firing techniques in
innovative ways. This piece shows his
characteristic vigour of approach to forms that
will work imaginatively with the firing.*

◐ **Lidded Vessel with Ears. Jeff Shapiro.**
Ceramic. Thrown and altered, anagama-fired.
12.5 x 38 x 38 cm (5 x 15 x 15 in). 1997

*This covered jar has its roots in Japanese tea
ceremony wares, the hallmark of which is an
affection for signs of either the process of
making or of usage.*

VESSELS
INTERPRETED

C LAY VESSELS are amongst the earliest known objects made by humans. Actual containers of food, water, wood or ashes, the mundane

and the precious, they have also always been on the threshold of

symbolic activities and rituals. They have been used to tell stories

and to express poetry. Vessels are rich metaphors for the human

body. Historically and culturally resonant, they are as full of possibility as ever.

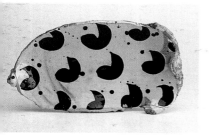

⬙ **Long Sashimi Plate. Katsue Ibata.**
Red clay, white slip, partial overglaze.
Thrown. Length 30 cm (12 in). 1994

*In classic slipware traditions, yellow and
brown colours of slip are used to create
geometric and repetitive patterns.
Ibata's work transforms this into extrovert
mark-making.*

◗ **(Untitled). Magdalene Odundo.** Reduced
red clay. 45.9 x 29.5 cm (18 x 11½ in). 1997

*Odundo's coiled vessels have gravitas. They
have a sense of condensed energy: the great
volume is held in tension by the sweep of the
neck and the wide elliptical opening. This
vessel could only be contemporary: its rich
visual echoes encompass not only African
ceramics but also early abstract art.*

Deep Blue Vessel. Gordon Baldwin. Multi-fired clay, oxides, stains and glazes. Hand-built. 36 x 35 x 33 cm (14 x 13¾ x 13 in). 1997

The depth of this blue is characteristic of Baldwin's work. His colours are more resonant with early Italian Renaissance painting than with ceramic history.

White Standing Vessel. Gordon Baldwin. Multi-fired clay, engobes, oxides, stains and glazes. Hand-built. 49 x 28 x 20 cm (19¼ x 11 x 8 in). 1998

All Baldwin's works are vessels. Often they have only the smallest of openings: their interiority is made even more powerful by our inability to see within.

White Vessel with Emergent Numerals. Gordon Baldwin. Multi-fired clay, engobes, oxides, stains and glazes. Hand-built. 21 x 49 x 40 cm (8¼ x 19¼ x 15¾ in). 1997

Baldwin conveys the powerful sense that his vessels have been part of an ageing process; that this present surface has many hidden layers beneath it. Like a palimpsest, where a text has been worked over and over again, the emergent numerals betray past histories and forgotten meanings.

Black Bowl with Piercings. Gordon Baldwin. Multi-fired clay, engobes, oxides, stains and glazes. Hand-built. 31 x 14 x 35 cm (12¼ x 16 x 13¾ in). 1997

With its pierced and scarified surface, this elliptical bowl form hovers between memories of functional vessels and natural forms.

◗ **Pale Double Pot with Black Drawing. Alison Britton.** Hand-built, high-fired earthenware, painted with slips and underglaze pigment under a clear matt glaze. 48 x 44 x 30 cm (19 x 17 x 12 in). 1995

Constructed from slabs of clay, Britton's ceramics are a matrix of angularity. There is no easy resting place for the eye as planes and lines shift without resolution.

◗ **Pot with Pleated Spout. Alison Britton.** Hand-built, high-fired earthenware, painted with slips and underglaze pigment under a clear matt glaze. 50 x 25 x 35 cm (19½ x 10 x 13½ in). 1997

Britton made her reputation with a series of porcelain jugs, often decorated with birds. There is a submerged anthropomorphism here with beak and eye still present.

◖ **Double Pot with Handles. Alison Britton.** Hand-built, high-fired earthenware, painted with slips and underglaze pigment under a clear matt glaze. 49 x 44 x 30 cm (19 x 17 x 12 in). 1996

Behind Britton's work lies the echo of American action painting. Slabs of clay are decorated with free gestural markings and trails of slips and pigments prior to being cut and formed. This gives her work an energy quite different from decorating a finished piece.

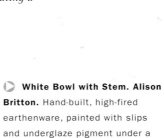 ◗ **White Bowl with Stem. Alison Britton.** Hand-built, high-fired earthenware, painted with slips and underglaze pigment under a clear matt glaze. 41 x 29 x 18 cm (16 x 11½ x 7 in). 1993

Domestic pots provide a fertile vocabulary of forms for the ceramic sculptor, as each form carries densely coded references to its function. Here Britton uses a bowl and stem, shapes that transmogrify into a ritualistic cup.

◯ **Vessel and Pedestal. David Roberts.**
T material, porcelain. Hand-built, raku-fired,
burnished slip interior, exterior ground and
polished post-firing. Length 45 cm (19¾ in).
1996

*The random interior crackle contrasts with the
restrained elliptical lines of the outside of this
quiet vessel.*

◯ **Two Black Vessels. David Roberts.**
T material, porcelain. Hand-built, raku-fired,
burnished; ground and polished interior.
27 x 32 x 16 cm (10¾ x 12½ x 6¼ in). 1997

*A burnished exterior surface has been eroded to
produce parallel lines suggestive of the strata of
rock or the ageing rings of trees.*

(Top) **Black-fired, Broken and Restored Bowl. Petrus Spronk.** Clay, gold leaf, iron oxide. Burnished, black-fired in wood kiln, smoke decorated shards, broken and restored. 23 x 45 cm (9 x 17¾ in). 1997

Broken after it had been wood-fired, then restored using gold leaf, the fractures and shards that make up this bowl play with images and ideas of mortality.

(Bottom) **Black-fired, Broken and Restored Bowl. Petrus Spronk.** Black-fired clay, gold leaf, red iron oxide. Burnished, wood-fired, broken and restored. 10 x 25 cm (4 x 10 in). 1997

This iridescent bowl reflects Spronk's experiences of walking through the Australian outback after a bush fire.

Hiffo 4. Pierre Bayle. Terracotta and slip. Height 40 cm (15¾ in). 1995

Overtly ritualistic in feel, raised off the ground by the three animal feet, this pot is little more than a simple canister. Yet with its surface marked by the terra sigillata slip, it looks towards the patination of bronzes, and to an indefinable sense of esoteric purpose. Clay has always been used to imitate other materials.

Gaea. Pierre Bayle. Terracotta. Terra sigillata. 30 x 30 cm (12 x 12 in). 1993

Bayle creates works of great articulation; they have perfect profiles and closely worked surfaces that seem close to metal. This highly ambiguous vessel is a disturbingly sexualized amalgam of the archaic and the futurist.

Pot Boule. Pierre Bayle. Terra sigillata. 1980s

In many ceramic traditions fired clay has creatively dissembled as wood, metal or stone. Here is a contemporary manifestation.

Canope. Pierre Bayle. Terra sigillata. Height 65 cm (25½ in). 1988

This vessel is like a fantasy of Orientalism. Even the finial is shaped like a Japanese sword.

(Untitled). **Magdalene Odundo.** Black terracotta. 36.5 x 43 cm (14½ x 17 in). 1997

(Untitled). **Magdalene Odundo.** Oxidized red clay. 69.5 x 33 cm (27¾ x 13¼ in). 1997

Odundo's vessels are coiled, then burnished, a process that gives them their dense surface. Odundo shows how it is possible for a maker to reinterpret forms that have been made countless times, and make them seem completely fresh.

(Untitled). **Magdalene Odundo.** Reduced red clay. 45.9 x 29.5 cm (18 x 11½ in).

Odundo is consummately skilled at creating dynamic forms, not just pleasing profiles. This work has memories of gourds and calabashes, but is also distinctly birdlike.

◐ Large Rust and Black Bowl. Robin Welch.
Reduced stoneware. Thrown, coiled and slab-built, black slip and porcelain slip, lustre glaze with salt wash, fired to 1300°C. 50 x 50 cm (20 x 20 in). 1997

With their abraded surfaces and rough edges, Welch's bowls display the energetic process of their making.

◑ Large White Bowl. Robin Welch.
Reduced stoneware. Thrown, coiled and slab-built, white porcelain slip, black slip and velvet colours, thin salt wash, fired to 1300°C. 50 x 50 cm (20 x 20 in). 1997

Welch transforms the kinds of marks made by chance in a wood-fired kiln into free and powerful brushwork. It is as if an abstract expressionist was painting a version of a Japanese pot.

◐ Oval Bottle Vase. Robin Welch.
Reduced stoneware. Slab and coil-built, white porcelain slip and lustre glaze, fired to 1300°C, re-fired to 1000°C with velvet colours and copper oxide. 60 x 40 x 25 cm (24 x 16 x 10 in). 1998

Though slab-built and coiled, this jar shares a relaxed and gestural approach to making with some traditions of Japanese thrown pottery.

Jar. Elspeth Owen. Grogged clay and porcelain slip. Pinched and burnished, low-fired. Height 25 cm (10 in). 1995

Fired surrounded by an unconventional array of materials, including seaweed, the surfaces of these pots look as though they have been aged.

Flecked Pot. Elspeth Owen. Coarsely grogged dark clay with porcelain slip. Pinched and burnished, low-fired. Height 15 cm (6 in). 1994

Owen makes pots of deceptive simplicity. She uses the basic making techniques of pinching and burnishing, yet her pots evoke strong and complex reactions when handled.

Bowl. Elspeth Owen. White grogged clay, coloured slips. Pinched and burnished, low-fired. Height 24 cm (9½ in). 1997

Owen's pinched bowls have an ethereal quality that derives not just from their physical lightness but also from their visual relationship to a range of insubstantial natural objects like leaves or lichen.

Left to right: **Quartet: Spout Pot "Red Moon", Gravity Vase, Counterpoint Vase, Spout Pot "Osiris". Elizabeth Fritsch.** Stoneware clay, stoneware slips. Hand-built, four colour firings. Max. height 44.5 cm (17½ in). 1990-91

Misplaced from another world, Fritsch's pieces encourage but resist interpretation. Often elliptical, they play with our assumptions of three-dimensionality.

Left to right: **Trio: Vase from Tlön, Lachrymatory, Vase "Double Fault". Elizabeth Fritsch.** Stoneware clay, stoneware slips. Hand-built, 5 colour firings. Heights 30 cm (12 in), 29.5 cm (11¾ in), 28 cm (11 in). 1984-88

The depth of colouring here is close to that of frescoes. The power of such work lies partly in this density: as the eye cannot register or focus on the surface, the vessels seem almost to lack substance.

Trio of Blown Away Vases: **"Collision of Particles: Parents and Child." Elizabeth Fritsch.** Stoneware clay, stoneware slips. Hand-built, 4 colour firings. Heights 48 cm (19 in), 41 cm (16 in), 61 cm (24 in). 1994

A joining of ideas and images derived from physics, this group creates a powerful impression of the dispersal of energy. Much of Fritsch's work is informed by her interest in how patterns, whether atomic or musical, can be understood.

◖ Left to right: **Polished Blue Pot with Haloed Flash, Slate Blue Pot with Haloed Rim. Jennifer Lee.** Coloured stoneware, T material, oxides. Hand-built, pinched and coiled, oxidation cone 9, left piece polished after firing. Left: 22.5 x 12 cm (9 x 4¾ in). Right: 14.5 x 11.5 cm (5¾ x 4½ in). 1997, 1996

Lee works with great and severe economy to make vessels that project a feeling of concentrated energy. Her pieces are pinched and coiled using a spectrum of coloured clays, then abraded and burnished.

◗ **Smoky Pot with Haloed Bands and Flat Shelf Rim. Jennifer Lee.** Coloured stoneware, T material, oxides. Hand-built, pinched and coiled, oxidation cone 9. 19.5 x 12.1 cm (7¾ x 4¾ in). 1993

Visually reminiscent of stratified rock, Lee's vessels have a distinctive weight and balance that are closer to that of archaic hand tools than natural forms.

Speckled Dark Pots. Jennifer Lee. Coloured stoneware. Hand-built, pinched and coiled, oxidation cone 9. Left: 17.2 x 12.1 cm (6¾ x 4¾ in). Right: 30.8 x 18 cm (12 x 7 in). 1997

With vessels that have this minimal sensibility, much depends on proportion and an exacting sense of tonality.

Bowl. Duncan Ross. Earthenware clay.
Burnished terra sigillata, inlaid and resist
decoration, smoke fired. Height 17 cm
(6¾ in). 1998

*One of the pleasures of repetition in decoration is the fulfilment or denial of
expectations: it makes you look at the whole object. Ross is a highly
accomplished inventor of complex patterns.*

Small Bowl. Duncan Ross.
Earthenware clay. Burnished
terra sigillata, inlaid and resist
decoration, smoke-fired. Height
12.5 cm (5 in). 1997

*Ross makes bowls that look
towards Native American
traditions, but have an almost
Art Deco gusto to them. The
smoke-firing gives them their
pleasingly subtle changes in
colour.*

Triptyque 2. Roseline Delisle. Porcelain. Thrown. Height 23 cm (9 in). 1991

This clutch of conflicting geometric forms brought together in a single vessel demonstrates Delisle's fascination with line and profile.

L'Ogive 10. Roseline Delisle. Porcelain. Thrown. 37 x 14 cm (14½ x 5½ in). 1986

Exactly banded colour produces a mesmerizing effect. Her work, like that of Fritsch, seems to ask for fictional explanations.

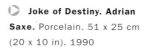

High-Fibre Earth-Quake Predicting ML. Adrian Saxe. Earthenware, stoneware, mixed media. 37 x 27 cm (14½ x 10¾ in). 1997

This is a sort of dysfunctional Aladdin's lamp atop a strange geological fragment. Saxe manages to make vessels that resonate with historical artefacts, but are also a disturbing and ironic contemporary commentary.

Joke of Destiny. Adrian Saxe. Porcelain. 51 x 25 cm (20 x 10 in). 1990

A Rococo gourd, mounted on an Oriental base, graffitied and flanked by cartoon ears, Saxe's porcelain vessel is a witty comment on eighteenth-century European court taste.

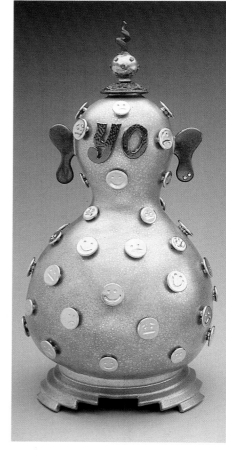

Deterministic Non-linear Flow. Adrian Saxe. Porcelain, mixed media. 48 x 33 cm (19 x 13 in). 1992

Saxe translates natural forms into Baroque extravaganzas of the display of skill. This puts him into a continuum of ceramic artists going back to the Italian Renaissance.

Tutti Frutti Bumper Car Jug. Kate Malone. Ceramic multiple fired earthenware. Press-moulded, hand-sprigged, glaze fired six times. 30 x 38 cm (12 x 15 in). 1997-98

This jug, with its lipstick colours, is a loving homage to the American culture of stylized cars and Krazy Kat cartoons. It is also redolent of the fairground: like a trophy from a sideshow.

Pumpkin Tea Pot. Kate Malone. Ceramic stoneware, crystalline glazes. Hand-coiled, modelled and built. 28 x 44 cm (11 x 17½ in). 1997

Often reminiscent of the Baroque ceramics of the Victorian period, Malone's pieces seem not to satirize but to relish their love of display.

Twin Gourds. Kate Malone. Ceramic stoneware, crystalline glazes. Press-moulded, coiled, hand-built. 40 x 30 cm (16 x 12 in). 1996-97

A combination of making techniques goes into the construction of Malone's pots. Press-moulded sections are used as the basis for further modelling and coiling: her finished pots retain a sense of growth.

Mother Pumpkin Box. Kate Malone. Ceramic, stoneware, crystalline glazes. Press-moulded and hand-modelled. 56 x 50 cm (22¼ x 20 in). 1995-98

Malone uses glazes in an expressive way. Her pots catch the way in which glazes flux, crystallize and melt in firings in such a way that the process seems to be continuing.

VESSELS INTERPRETED

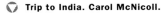 **Tea for One. Carol McNicoll.**
High-fired earthenware. Slip-cast teapot and found cup. Height 20 cm (8 in). 1997

This slipcast teapot was designed to provide sanctuary for odd cups found in junk shops. Acting as an impromptu plinth, swathed in bandages or scarves, it also looks in need of help.

 Trip to India. Carol McNicoll.
High-fired earthenware. Assembled from slip-cast elements decorated with transfers, coloured slips and glazes. Height 40 cm (16 in). 1998

Assembled from disparate slipcast elements, this piece is a ceramic travelogue. Textiles the colour of the earth and transfers of a sacred cow jostle for attention in a characteristically extrovert work.

(Top) **Oval Curbside Teapot (variation # 12) - Yixing series. Richard Notkin.** Stoneware. Cast and assembled. 8.5 x 20.5 x 10 cm (3¼ x 8 x 3¾ in). 1990

(Middle) **Light Bulb Teapot (variation # 9) – Yixing series. Richard Notkin.** Stoneware. Cast and assembled. 12.5 x 16.5 x 9.5 cm (5 x 6½ x 3¾ in). 1990

(Bottom) **Nuclear Nuts Teapot – Yixing series. Richard Notkin.** Stoneware. Thrown and cast elements. 12.5 x 16 x 10 cm (4¾ x 6¼ x (3¾ in). 1990

Notkin's work is a vivid contemporary use of the Chinese high-fired red stoneware tradition of Yixing. This tradition is characterized by the density of the unglazed surface, similar to masonry in touch, and the extravagant imagination of the forms (including architectural and natural) that were made from this material.

Notkin extends a basic vocabulary of Yixing shapes into a run of visual puns. Vessels, always "carriers" or "containers" of meaning, here become a container of electrical energy, even a source of nuclear fusion.

With cartoon-like energy emanating from spout and handle, these complex vessels show how politicized ceramics can be.

99

Large Platter. Katsue Ibata. Red clay, white slip, partial overglaze. ⌀ 60 cm (24 in). 1991

Energetic punctuation marks of slip decoration are scattered over Ibata's work. She takes the European tradition of slip decoration and treats it with a completely different sensibility. There is a hidden memory of a heraldic dish here.

Long Sashimi Plate. Katsue Ibata. Red clay, white slip, partial overglaze. Length 30 cm (12 in). 1994

Treating clay with abandon, Ibata cuts, inscribes and tears the edges of her slabbed dishes to give them a feeling of having been part of larger forms.

Sgraffito Plate.
Kim Hono. Stoneware with sgraffito. Ø 22 cm (8¾ in). 1998

Dry, grainy textures that have a close affinity to stone give Hono's work its particular resonance. They are as close to the studied "primitivism" of a painter like Dubuffet as to Korean vernacular ceramics.

Three Beakers.
Kim Hono. Red terracotta clay. Thrown. Height 12 cm (4¾ in). 1997

These simple upright bowls are treated with a lightness of touch. Both making and decorating share the same freedom in mark making.

REINVENTING THE WHEEL

T HE FAMILY OF POTS MADE on the wheel may share some

characteristics, but not many. As a family it contains vessels retaining free

throwing marks and vessels where all traces of the hand have

been effaced, pots thrown quickly and painstakingly made pots.

Overtly functional pots and covertly metaphorical ones are all

made on the wheel. These are well-established methods and

principles, what is new is the sense of the reinvigoration of an

ancient technique: an investigation into the dynamic pulse of thrown clay.

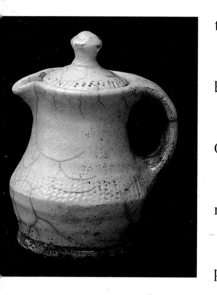

◐ Jug. Inger Rokkjær. Thrown, raku-fired.
Height 13 cm (5¼ in). 1993

*The broad splayed base of this lidded jar is
reminiscent of medieval pottery but the
robustness of form is belied by the luminosity
of the glaze.*

◑ Teapot on Stand. Walter Keeler.
Whieldonware. 1060°C. Height 18 cm (7 in). 1998

*Just as Keeler throws and then deconstructs his
pots before reassembling them, so they can be
seen as a deconstruction of ceramic traditions
and their reformation into ambiguous
contemporary objects.*

◗ **Beaked Jug.**
Jeff Oestreich. Thrown and altered, soda-fired. Height 19 cm (7½ in). 1998

Everything about this fiercely beaked jug is suggestive of forward energy. Constructed like the prow of a ship, it seems to enact the movement of pouring liquid.

▽ **Platter.**
Jeff Oestreich. Thrown and altered, soda-fired. ∅ 39 cm (15½ in). 1998

Oestreich's subtle palette of colour is derived from the soda firing, in which he uses copper to give greys, greens and turquoises.

▽ **Vase.**
Jeff Oestreich. Stoneware. Thrown and altered, soda-fired. Height 18 cm (7 in). 1998

This thrown and constructed form with its splayed foot, geometrical patterning and whimsical applied wings looks back to the Art Deco ceramics of the 1920s.

Covered Jar. Chris Staley.
Stoneware. Height 36 cm (14 in).
1993

Chinese pots of the T'ang dynasty used a similar decorative technique. Keeping a form of this rotundity from seeming too facile is a matter of providing subtle definition at the rim.

Teapot. Chris Staley.
Stoneware. Height 20.5 cm (8 in).
1991

This teapot is an elegant disposition of shallow curves. The space under the handle has visual weight and here it balances the volume of the teapot body.

Porcelain Bowl. Ryoji Koie. Porcelain. Thrown.
⌀ 28.9 cm (11½ in). 1998

*The sweeping shifts in volume of this bowl are held in
check by the inscribed lines – more marks or ciphers of
erasure or defacement than conventional decoration. Here
the exterior of an unglazed, high-fired porcelain bowl, with
a dense quality not dissimilar to that of stone, is contrasted
with a simple transparent-glazed, white interior.*

Devil Jumping Teabowl. Ryoji Koie. Stoneware. Height
11.5 cm (4½ in). 1991

*Unlike many Westerners working in Japanese ceramic
idioms, Koie holds no particular brief for specific historical
styles but works across many traditions. Behind this
teabowl is an Oribe tradition of the effacement of a pattern
by partly dipping a pot in a strong-coloured glaze.*

Salaam – Salaam (Medium). Ryoji Koie.
Stoneware. Slab-built. 27.5 x 25 cm
(10¾ x 10 in). 1991

*A slab of clay, scarred, inscribed and
punctured, resting on four disparate thrown
feet, makes up this piece. A sort of
dysfunctional dish for offerings, it is a
powerful example of how vessels can work
with the symbolic language of function and
become ambiguous and disturbing objects.*

Sugar Bowl. Will Levi Marshall.
Oxidized stoneware (1280°C) with lustre
(750°C). Thrown and altered, glazes
poured using masking and wax resist.
Height 10 cm (4 in). 1998

*Levi Marshall adds an attenuated
handle to this lidded bowl, displaying a
relish for pushing out the conventions
of visual balance.*

Two Mugs. Will Levi Marshall. Oxidized stoneware (1280°C) with
lustre (750°C). Thrown and altered, glazes poured using masking and
wax resist. Height 12 cm (4½ in). 1998

*The form of these two mugs, though thrown, is similar to that of
metal tankards. The application of gold lustre adds to the play of
ideas on the relative values of materials – lavishness applied to a
humble object.*

Salt Glazed Teapot. Jane Hamlyn. Stoneware. Salt glazed, wheel-thrown, modelled handles, press-moulded spout, cobalt and titanium slips. 28 x 30 cm (11 x 12 in). 1998

With a distant memory of oil cans in the sharpness and clarity of the thrown and altered body, this teapot is a homage to the ways in which clay and metal have influenced each other. The tense curlicues of the handles are like shavings from a lathe.

Serving Dish. Jane Hamlyn. Stoneware. Salt glazed, thrown sides, slabbed base, modelled handles. 10 x 35 x 30 cm (4 x 14 x 12 in). 1998

There is a certain grandeur in this serving dish. The subtle tension at work between the oval form and the flared rim keeps the eye moving.

 **Salt Glazed Jar. Jane Hamlyn.** Stoneware. Salt glazed, thrown, modelled handle, cobalt and titanium slips. 35 x 25 cm (14 x 10 in). 1998

Hamlyn's pots carry an informed sense of ceramic tradition. Her use of salt glaze is particularly expressive, often reminiscent of English and German vernacular pottery.

Bowl. Janice Tchalenko. High-fired reduced stoneware. Thrown, with coloured glaze painting. 15.5 x 31.5 cm (6¼ x 12¼ in). 1996

Tchalenko radically extended the palette of glaze colours used by studio potters. In so doing, she opened up neglected aspects of ceramic history, such as the work of the sixteenth-century potter, Bernard Palissy, for reappraisal.

Bowl. Janice Tchalenko. High-fired reduced stoneware. Thrown and impressed. 7 x 29 cm (3 x 11½ in). 1998

Full of movement, this vortex of competing undulations is typical of Tchalenko's enjoyment of the process of flux in throwing and in glazing.

Bowl. Janice Tchalenko. High-fired reduced stoneware. Thrown and impressed. 12 x 32 cm (4¾ x 12½ in). 1998

Inverting normal expectations about the interiors of vessels, this bowl has a raised surface on the inside.

Vase Form. **Sutton Taylor.** Ceramic lustreware. Height 51 cm (20 in). 1997

An exactitude of internal and external profile acts as counterfoil to Taylor's broadly decorative use of lustre.

Platter. **Sutton Taylor.** Ceramic lustreware. ⌀ 51 cm (20 in). 1997

Taylor makes bowls of an ethereal lightness. As his lustred surfaces relate to naturally variegated patterns like autumnal leaves, this makes for a strange tactile parallel between natural and thrown forms.

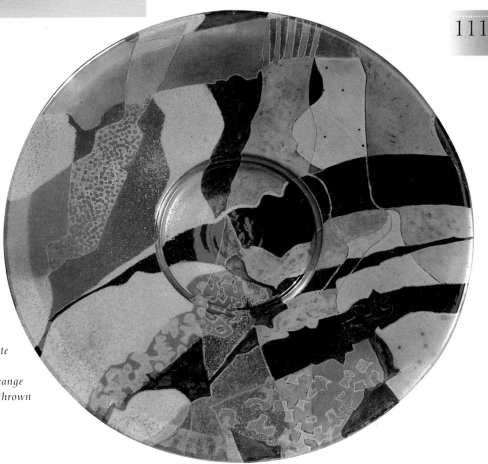

Teapot on Stand. Walter Keeler.
Whieldonware, cream earthenware, coloured lead glazes. Biscuit fired at 1145°C, glaze fired at 1060°C. Height 20.5 cm (8 in). 1998

Eighteenth-century Staffordshire pottery, with its tortoiseshell glazes and crabstick spouts, is the source of reference for this teapot. Keeler's interpretation of historic ceramics is incisive and robust.

Jug on Pedestal. Walter Keeler.
Whieldonware, earthenware. Height 20.5 cm (8 in). 1998

By integrating this jug with a grandiose plinth, Keeler comments wryly on the manner in which domestic objects are appraised and valued.

Salt Glaze Teapot. Walter Keeler. Earthenware. Height 23 cm (9 in). 1998

Reassembled from thrown components, Keeler's saltglaze teapots show a similar complex interrogation of traditions as his Whieldonware. Distended and angular, these forms carry echoes of industrial artefacts.

Salt Glaze Jug. Walter Keeler. Earthenware. Height 25 cm (10 in). 1998

Saltglaze is used to create the mottled "orange peel" effect on this large tilted jug.

Teapot, Pourer and Cup. Kevin White. Wheel-thrown and altered. Heights: cup: 7.8 cm (3¼ in); teapot: 18.5 cm (7¼ in); pourer: 7.8 cm (3¼ in). 1996

Softly distorted after throwing, these pots are inviting to the hand. Function is not seen as a constraint but as a challenging starting point for invention.

Vessel. Kevin White. Limoges porcelain. Wheel-thrown and altered. 26 x 16 cm (10¼ x 6¼ in). 1997

White utilizes an under-glaze blue and on-glaze enamels to complex decorative effect. The dramatic juxtaposition of undecorated areas creates an impression of fractured movement.

Bowl. Kevin White. Limoges Porcelain. Wheel-thrown and altered, decorated in underglaze blue. 15 x 44 cm (6 x 17½ in). 1996

A finely thrown, flared form provides a necessarily clear surface for this intricate patterning.

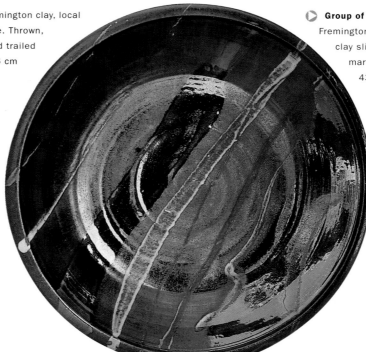

Platter. Clive Bowen. Fremington clay, local coloured clay slips, clear glaze. Thrown, decorated with poured slip and trailed slip, wood-fired, 1060°C. ∅ 46 cm (18 in). 1998

Genuine spontaneity, rather than the contrived attempt or the merely haphazard, is easy to discern. It is present here in Bowen's work.

Group of Tall Jugs. Clive Bowen. Fremington earthenware clay, local coloured clay slips, clear glaze. Slip-trailed and marked with the thumb. Height 30 and 43 cm (12 and 17 in). 1998

Sturdy and broad-based, these jugs owe a debt to medieval English baluster pitchers: the tradition from which the strap handle springs. Undulating throwing rings are held in check by the deep profile and resolution of the top edge.

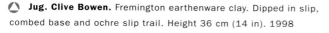

Jug. Clive Bowen. Fremington earthenware clay. Dipped in slip, combed base and ochre slip trail. Height 36 cm (14 in). 1998

Vernacular pottery lies behind much of Bowen's work, but the freedom of the trailed slip decoration looks as much to action painting as to peasant traditions.

Large Store Jar. Clive Bowen. Fremington earthenware clay, local coloured clay slips, clear glaze. Dipped in white slip, design drawn with a stick (combed). Height 41 cm (16 in). 1998

This lidded jar retains echoes of Oriental pottery while remaining grounded in traditions of English slipware.

▶ **Yellow Cylinder. Inger Rokkjær.**
Thrown and cut. Raku-fired.
23 x 11.4 cm (9 x 4½ in). 1992

Seemingly unstudied, Rokkjær's raku-fired ceramics are quiet and subtle in effect. The chance marks of crackle and scorching from the raku firing are not allowed to overwhelm.

△ **Softly Thrown Dish. Sandy Brown.**
Stoneware. Thrown and painted with strong cobalt oxides and copper-green glazes. Ø 52 cm (20½ in). 1997

◁ **Softly Thrown Dish. Sandy Brown.**
Stoneware. Thrown and painted with coloured glazes. Ø 50 cm (19¾ in). 1997

Brown uses brushes of varying thickness, even employing ones made for house paint, to build up her patterns. Whilst looking completely spontaneous, there is usually a hidden decorative structure.

◀ **Mycenaean – Yourcenaean # 3. Steven Glass.** Porcelain. Wheel-thrown, polychrome engobe painting and template transfer; fired in oxidation to cone 7, independent pedestal base. 48 x 25.5 x 21 cm (19 x 10 x 8½ in). 1989

A graffitied version of a Mycenaean vase, this exuberant piece substitutes bold abstraction for representation.

⬡ **Bottle. Steven Glass.** White stoneware. Wheel-thrown, polychrome engobe painting, sgraffito drawing, glazed and fired in oxidation to cone 7. 28 x 18 x 18 cm (11 x 7 x 7 in). 1997

A cluster of different decorative techniques has been brought together on the surface of this bottle. The combination of slips, to produce broad colour washes, with sgraffito, to give line, is most effective.

▶ **Mycenaean – Yourcenaean # 2. Steven Glass.** Porcelain. Wheel-thrown, polychrome engobe painting and template transfer. Black glaze fired to cone 7 in oxidation. 30.5 x 37 x 28 cm (12 x 14½ x 11 in). 1989

Whimsical additions to this thrown pedestal bowl give it a sense of ambiguity: it hovers on the edge of post-modern historical pastiche.

Porcelain Bowl. Greg Daly. Porcelain, resin lustres. Thrown. 11 x 12.5 cm (4½ x 5 in). 1993

Daly is concerned with the play of light on surfaces. The iridescence of the multi-layered lustres creates a strange and shifting tonality, where the same piece seems to have different depths in different lights.

Decorated Platter. Greg Daly. Stoneware. Thrown, glaze-on-glaze, 1300°C. Ø 48 cm (19 in). 1997

A play on negative and positive space, the glaze-on-glaze line animates the background of this platter.

Lustre Decorated Platter. Greg Daly. Stoneware. Thrown, glaze-on-glaze, resin lustres. Ø 95 cm (37 in). 1996

This large platter shows Daly's graphic strengths: a powerful linear interruption of lustred decoration giving a dynamism to the whole piece.

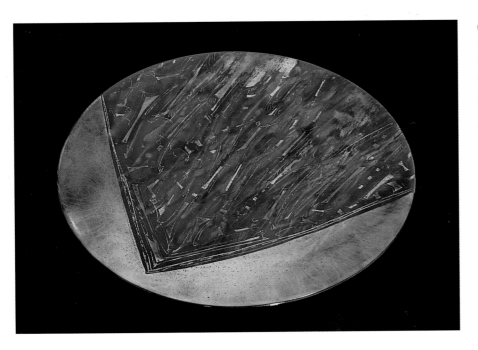

REINVENTING THE WHEEL

Mentori Vase. Shiro Tsujimura. Stoneware with feldspar and ash. Anagama-fired. Height 30 cm (12 in). 1993

Two conflicting movements hold this vase in tension: one the throwing of an extremely thick cylinder and the other the dynamic cutting movement of the turning. The top of this vase gives a feeling of abandonment rather than closure of process.

● **Oribe Cylindrical Teabowl. Shiro Tsujimura.**
Stoneware. Green slight brush decoration.
⌀ 12.5 cm (5 in). 1993

*Teabowls are imbued with great significance
in Japan: a nexus of functional, historical
and symbolic meanings. This teabowl is
contemplative, the severe profile modulated
by the gently pitted surface.*

● **Kohiki Summer Teabowl. Shiro Tsujimura.**
Stoneware. ⌀ 17 cm (6¾ in). 1993

*Learning to "read" pots from diverse cultural
traditions is a complex task. Slight deviations
from norms, or modulations of conventions, can
make apparently simple pots, like this teabowl of
Tsujimura's, quietly subversive. Tsujimura is a
master of this play with tradition.*

ENDPIECE

Contemporary pots, ceramics that were made in this century,

have diverse lives, live in many different places. And where we

find them can often radically alter our ways of understanding and

approaching them. Are they shown with lots of room around them?

Behind glass? Open to the touch? We can find them in studios and

workshops, clean or dusty, stacked up or carefully tended. We find

them in people's homes: on mantelpieces, in display cases, filled

with flowers or specially put aside, part of everyday life on the

draining board, outside in the garden or on the floor for the dog.

Porcelain Cup and Saucer. Julian Stair.

They live in museums and in grand collections alongside the

historical collections that inspired them. In this context we can look

Cargo No. 2. Edmund de Waal

at them and see where particular ideas

and influences came from, feel the

currents of tradition and innovation

ebbing and flowing into modern

ceramic work.

They live in craft galleries, exhibited

124

and displayed alongside examples of craftwork in other media, such as metal, glass, wood or cloth. In this context we are made aware of how makers of a similar generation approach and cross-reference their materials.

And, of course, ceramics are the neighbours of contemporary sculpture and fine art: in this context they have gravitas and seriousness. The flow of energy between contemporary arts is most manifest here: the shared concerns with ideas of installation, or indeed the shared interrogation of ideas of gender and politics.

Ceramics cross people's lives in manifold ways, looked at, collected and used. And just as the people who make these ceramic objects do not obey any easy prescriptive image, so the ways in which they talk about themselves is varied and rich. There are artists. There are potters and ceramicists, ceramists and makers, artists in clay, and artist–craftsmen. The myriad ways that those who use clay define themselves, the places and ways in which they show their work, and the history of ceramics to which they ascribe themselves, tell us that these ceramics can be wonderful and beautiful and affecting. And that they are not, perhaps, as easy as they seem at first sight.

△ **Joke of Destiny. Adrian Saxe.**

INDEX OF ARTISTS

The artists featured in this book are listed here in alphabetical order. The pages on which their work appears follow each entry.

C: Commissions accepted
W: Workshops
V: Visits to the studio **by appointment only**

Will Levi Marshall
Orchardton Pottery
Auchencairn
Castle Douglas
Dumfries & Galloway
DG7 1QL
Scotland, UK
Tel: 01556 640 399
Fax: 01556 640 116
will.phoebe@btinternet.com
C; W; V
page 108

Kate Malone
157 Balls Pond Road
London N1 4BG, UK
Tel: 020 7254 4037
Fax: 020 7275 0401
C; W; V
pages 96, 97

Carol McNicoll
3 Charlton Kings Road
London NW5 2SB, UK
Tel: 020 7482 2205
Fax: 020 7482 2204
C; V
page 98

Richard T. Notkin
c/o Garth Clark Gallery
W
page 99

Magdalene Odundo
c/o Anthony Slayter-Ralph
P.O. Box 61
Santa Barbara
California 93102, USA
Tel: 805 969 5565
Fax: 805 962 2924
artemax@aol.com
W
pages 75, 84, 85

Jeff Oestrich
c/o Contemporary Ceramics
7 Marshall Street
London W1V 1LP, UK
Tel/Fax: 020 7437 7605
page 104

Elspeth Owen
79 Broadway
Grantchester
Cambridge CB3 9NQ, UK
Tel: 01223 841 297
C; W; V
page 87

Grayson Perry
27 Wilmington Square
London WC1X 0EG, UK
Tel: 020 8519 7425
C; V
page 46, 58, 59

Sara Radstone
c/o Barrett Marsden Gallery
V
pages 62, 63

David Roberts
Cressfield House
44 Upperthong Lane
Holmfirth, Huddersfield
West Yorks HD7 1BQ, UK
Tel: 01484 685 110
david@davidroberts-ceramics.com
http://www.davidroberts-ceramics.com
W; V
page 80

Pilar Rojas
34 Rankins Road
Kensington
VIC 3031, Australia
Tel: 03 9376 4143
C; W; V
page 44

Inger Rokkjaer
c/o Galerie Besson
pages 102, 119

Duncan Ross
Daneshay House
Alma Lane
Hale, Farnham
Surrey
GU9 0LT
UK
Tel/Fax: 01252 710 704
V
page 92

Adrian Saxe
c/o Garth Clark Gallery
pages 94, 95

Jeff Shapiro
62 Raycliff Drive
Accord
NY 12404
USA
Tel/Fax: 914 626 0684
jeshapi@juno.com
C; W; V
page 73

Alev Ebüzziya Siesbye
c/o Galerie Besson
pages 1, 14, 15

Richard Slee
c/o Barrett Marsden Gallery
C, W
pages 56, 57

Martin Smith
c/o Barrett Marsden Gallery
pages 40, 41

Rupert Spira
Church Farm
Bishops Castle
More
Shropshire
SY9 5HH, UK
Tel/Fax: 01588 650 588
C; V
page 19

Petrus Spronk
PO Box 69
Hepburn Springs
VIC 3461
Australia
Tel/Fax: 03 5348 3467
petrus@hello.com.au
C; W; V
page 81

Julian Stair
127 Court Lane
London
SE21 7EE, UK
Tel/Fax: 020 8693 4877
C; V
pages 9, 28, 29, 124

Chris Staley
c/o Garth Clark Gallery
page 105

Sutton Taylor
c/o Hart Gallery
113 Upper Street
London
N1 1QN, UK
Tel: 020 7704 1131
Fax: 020 7704 1707
page 111

Janice Tchalenko
30 Therapia Road
London
SE22 0SE, UK
Tel/Fax: 020 8516 3489
j-t@dircon.co.uk
C; V
page 110

Vladimir Tsivin
c/o Galerie Besson
page 51

Prue Venables
27 Orchard Crescent
North Box Hill
Melbourne
VIC 3129, Australia
Tel: 03 9857 6393
Fax: 03 9857 7339
iang@melbpc.org.au
C; W; V
pages 30, 31

Irene Vonck
c/o Gallery de Witte Voet
Kerkstraat 135
1017 GE Amsterdam
The Netherlands
Tel: 020 625 8412
brovo@ibm.net
C; V
pages 60, 65

Robin Welch
Stradbroke
Eye
Suffolk IP21 5JP, UK
Tel: 01379 384 416
C; W; V
page 86

Kevin White
29 Perth Street
Prahran
VIC 3181, Australia
Tel: 03 9529 8930
Fax: 03 9925 3731
C; V
pages 114, 115

Takeshi Yasuda
37 Kensington Gardens
Bath
Avon BA1 6LH, UK
Tel: 01225 334 136
Fax: 01225 313 492
Takeshi@dial.pipex.com
C; W; V
pages 4, 12, 13

Masamichi Yoshikawa
F479-0832
4-65 Haramatsu-cho
Tokoname City
Aichi-Ken, Japan
Tel/Fax: 0569 346 800
C; V
pages 35, 39

Galleries and Representatives:

Barrett Marsden Gallery
17-18 Great Sutton Street
London EC1V 0DN, UK
Tel: 020 7336 6396
Fax: 020 7336 6391
barrettmarsden@bmgallery.co.uk

Galerie Besson
15 Royal Arcade
28 Old Bond Street
London W1X 3HB, UK
Tel: 020 7491 1706
Fax: 020 7495 3203
anita@galeriebesson.co.uk

The Crafts Council
44a Pentonville Road
London N1 9BY, UK
Tel: 020 7278 7700
Fax: 020 7837 6891

Garth Clark Gallery
24 West 57th Street, #305
New York
NY 10019, USA
Tel: 212 246 2205
Fax: 212 489 5168

Andrew Redman
38 Cornwall Road
London SE1 8TJ, UK
Tel: 020 7928 0739
Fax: 020 7207 5108

GLOSSARY OF POTTERY TERMS

Anagama kiln *A single-chambered, wood-fired Japanese kiln.*

Burnishing *Rubbing a hard, smooth object, such as a spoon or pebble, across a leather-hard pot in order to polish it.*

Celadon *A green to blue-grey stoneware or porcelain glaze, originally from China. The colour is derived from the use of iron in reduction firing.*

Creamware *Cream coloured earthenware, first used in the eighteenth century.*

Earthenware *Low-fired pottery, often with a greater degree of porosity than stoneware.*

Grog *Ground up fired clay, added to give texture or to help in the forming of the pot.*

On-glaze *Ceramic colours placed on top of a fired glaze surface and then given an additional firing.*

Pinching *Forming a pot between fingers and thumb.*

Plasticity *The ability of a clay body to be solid and yet hold water.*

Porcelain *A clay body, high in kaolin, that fires white and can be translucent.*

Press-moulding *A way of making pots by pressing slabs of clay onto plaster moulds.*

Raku *A low-fired Japanese technique that centres on taking red hot pots from the kiln and cooling them in various substances.*

Reduction firing *Reduced oxygen firing.*

Saggar *A way of protecting pots from direct contact with flames by placing them in refractory boxes.*

Sgraffito *Decoration formed by scratching through one slip or glaze to reveal another.*

Slip-casting *Liquid clay or slip is poured in moulds to form pots.*

Stoneware *Pottery usually fired above 1200°C (2192°F).*

T material *A very refractory white stoneware clay containing a coarse molochite. Good for hand-building.*

Terra sigillata *An extremely fine ball clay, partially sintered, fired to a semi-sheen.*

Terracotta *From the Italian for "fired earth", it simply signifies red earthenware.*

Under-glaze *Ceramic colours usually applied to a biscuit fired pot, covered with a transparent glaze and refired.*

Whieldonware *An eighteenth century kind of marbled or tortoiseshell decorated earthenware.*

Dimensions
Where one measurement is given, the relevant dimension is indicated in the text. Two measurements are listed in the order height x width; three measurements are given as height x width x depth.

Acknowledgements

The author and the publisher would like to thank all the artists and in particular the following individuals and institutions for their kind assistance in the loan of transparencies and of ceramic work photographed for this book:

Bridgeman Art Library; Bonhams, London; Garth Clark Gallery; The Hart Gallery; Egg; Galerie Besson; Contemporary Ceramics; Jill Fanshawe Kato; Sara Radstone; Andrew Redman; Terra Keramiek and Claire Thorn.

The Long Sashimi Plates on pages 74 and 100 (bottom) are from the collection of Jill Fanshawe Kato.

We have made every effort to acknowledge everyone and apologise if, in error, anyone has been omitted.

Photography credits

Noel Allum/Garth Clark Gallery 45; John Andow 118; Ian Auld 70 tr; James Austin 87; Russel Baader 121; Bob Barrett 73; David Beard 43; Jenny Beavan 64; Galerie Besson 10, 61, 102, 107, 119; David Binns 34; Terence Bogue 30, 31, 44, 114, 115; Thomas Bohle 36 m, 36 b, 37 b; Bonhams, London, UK 24, 40, 41; Stephen Brayne 8, 16, 96; Alison Brown 72; Marc Burden 116, 117; G. Carr 22; Mogens Carrebye 1, 14; Jenni Carter 21; Chris Chapman 66; Courtesy of Garth Clark Gallery 25, 45, 93, 94, 95, 99, 105; Joanna Constantinidis 18; David Cripps 43, 54, 55, 78, 79, 88, 98, 110; M. di Bartolomeo 65; Ken Eastman 42, 43; Joel Fildes 50; Michael Flynn 4, 47, 53; Victor France 72; Geoffrey Fuller 52; Hubert Gentry/Anton Gallery Washington, DC 11, 32, 33; Sebastian N. Gordon 124 b; Peter Greenhalf 48; Nicolette Hallett 87; Jane Hamlyn 109; Brian Hand 20; Jerry Hardman-Jones 80; The Hart Gallery 111; Michael Harvey 2, 14, 15, 17, 51, 68, 69, 90, 106, 122, 123; Michael Harvey/Galerie Besson 68; Matthew Hollow 96, 97; J. P Lefevre 82, 83; Will Levi Marshall 108; Jean-Jacques Morer 67; Sarah Morris 5, 89; Zul Mukhida 56, 57; Graham Murrell 86, 70, 71; Abbas Nazari 75, 84, 85; Grayson P 46, 58, 59; Mike Pocklington Inc. 120; Giles ' 124 t; William Robertson 9, 28, 29; John Rog 49; Duncan Ross 92; Lily Marie Rua 36 t, 37 t; John Russell 118; Phil Sayer 76, 77; Richard Slee 56, 57; Martin Smith 40; Petrus Spronk 81; Dewi Tannatt Lloyd 38; John Tchalenko 110; Luke Tchalenko 110; Gallery Ueda 67; Simon Upton 19; Irene Vonck 65; John White/Garth Clark Gallery 94; Takeshi Yasuda 12, 13.

This edition first published in 2003 by
New Holland Publishers (UK) Ltd
London · Cape Town · Sydney · Auckland

Garfield House, 86-88 Edgware Road
London W2 2EA
United Kingdom

80 McKenzie Street
Cape Town 8001
South Africa

Level 1, Unit 4, 14 Aquatic Drive
Frenchs Forest, NSW 2086
Australia

218 Lake Road
Northcote, Auckland
New Zealand

Copyright © 1999 in text Edmund de Waal
Copyright © 1999 in photography
New Holland Publishers (UK) Ltd with
the exception of those listed above
Copyright © 1999 New Holland Publishers (UK) Ltd

The right of Edmund de Waal to be identified as the author of this work has been asserted by him in accordance with the Copyright, Design and Patents Act, 1988.

ISBN 1 85974 223 8

Editorial Assistant: Anke Ueberberg
Designer: Grahame Dudley
Special Photography: Michael Harvey
Project Editor: Rosemary Wilkinson

Editorial Direction: Yvonne McFarlane

Reproduction by Modern Age Repro House, Hong Kong
Printed and bound in Singapore by Tien Wah Press (Pte) Ltd

2 4 6 8 10 9 7 5 3 1

For Ben, a picture book.

Author's Acknowledgements
I am most gratefully indebted to all the artists who contributed to the making of this book. Gretchen Adkins of the Garth Clark Gallery, New York, Jenny Macdiarmot and Emi Trowbridge of Galerie Besson, Juliana Barrett and Andrew Redman were patient and generous beyond any call of duty or friendship. To Julian Stair, ceramic interlocutor, I am happily indebted, and to my partner and clearest reader, Susan Chandler, I owe most of all.